Truth, Myth,

and Symbol

Truth, Myth, and Symbol

Edited by

THOMAS J. J. ALTIZER
WILLIAM A. BEARDSLEE
J. HARVEY YOUNG

Prentice-Hall, Inc. A SPECTRUM BOOK *Englewood Cliffs, N.J.*

For

Ernest Cadman Colwell

Preface

In our contemporary world is "truth" as a concept no longer valid, or does it have meaning and relevance? And how is the serious reader, encountering "symbol" and "myth" wherever he turns, to understand these terms?

The first half of this book concerns "truth"; the second half concerns "symbol" and "myth." This collection of essays represents a symposium of men trained in special fields of knowledge, each seeking to use his special competence for general enlightenment. In this interdisciplinary inquiry the participating scholars confront a common set of basic problems and strive to communicate to others their own particular insights and methods.

The problem of "truth" is confronted in the pages that follow by the philosopher, the physical chemist, the social theorist, the historian, and students of literature and religion. "Myth" and "symbol" are discussed by scholars of archaeology, religion, philosophy, literature, and social science, who report on the meanings and uses of these words in scholarship today.

Each author strives to convey his special knowledge in eminently readable language and with illustrations that the nonspecialist can comprehend. His first presentation, indeed, was before a live audience, with clarity called for by personal confrontation: the essays were written for delivery before a continuing seminar of Emory University's interdisciplinary doctoral program in the humanities and social sciences, the Institute of the Liberal Arts. Here students with many different "majors" in their college training face problems which all educated men confront—how to understand the specialist, how to talk with each other across the boundaries of disciplines, how to strive for what consensus there may be, how to grapple with sharp differences.

The Institute, begun in 1952, has as its purpose the training of scholars whose fields of special knowledge cross the borders of traditional disciplines. Many of its graduates, members of regular college departments, also now teach in the broad humanities courses required of freshmen and sophomores on many campuses. The education of Institute graduates requires some formal effort to get them, whatever their specialties, to talk with each other about broad problems of pertinence to all. It seems appropriate that this university effort may now serve to help the general reader, as well, to take a panoramic view along an important span of today's intellectual horizon.

Those who presented the papers on "truth," "symbol," and "myth"—somewhat revised for this book—spoke for themselves, not necessarily as spokesmen for their disciplines. Other literary critics, sociologists, historians, may differ in their analyses. A community of scholars on an American campus today, as Richard Hocking points out, does not share a unanimity of philosophical outlook.

The participants in this symposium acknowledge a debt of gratitude to the vision and leadership of the Institute of the Liberal Art's first director, Ernest Cadman Colwell, and express this appreciation in the dedication of this volume.

A special word of thanks is due Mrs. Martha McKay for her patient and careful typing and retyping of the manuscript.

Acknowledgments for quotations cited are given in the notes.

The idea of making a book for general readers from these papers originated with William Beardslee, then director of the Institute, who also performed the major portion of editing the manuscript before going to Germany as a Fulbright scholar. Thomas Altizer and I then jointly inherited the editorial mantle.

J. Harvey Young

Table of

Contents

The Problem

of Truth

The Problem of Truth

Richard Hocking

The inquiry which prompted these essays is daring, and also perennial; it is a testing of the confidence with which we devote ourselves to the advancement of learning. Whether in solitude or together, in laboratory or library or atelier, one of our silent assumptions, underlying the wide range of intellectual effort, is that knowledge can be, and is being, advanced. This advance we take to be at the same time an increase of truth.

Intellectual inquiry is compounded of curiosity, question, doubt, and critique. This is the normal state of mental life. Quite as normal is the reflective disposition to turn this curiosity and doubt back upon the very effort of inquiry itself. Then we ask: "What is truth?" "Can it be reached by our kind?" "Is there a favored method for doing so?" "By what criterion can we know that we know?"

In an especially analytic time like ours, these questions have grown radical in their depth. In communities like modern universities, the reflective doubt which prompts the questions may call in question the belief that truth has any common meaning in the diversity of disciplines: the natural sciences, human history, criticism of art and literature, theological doctrine. Without some common sense of truth, what sort of community can the modern university be, or, for that matter, any institution of learning?

It is an irony that, in the act of deepening our doubt about any common meaning of the word "truth," we often, indeed regularly, ground this doubt upon some principle which we undoubtingly hold, and hold to be sound and solid enough to support the cause of the advancement of learning. Truth is doubted from a base of some truth not doubted. This irony was experienced in an early phase of our civilization, and was personified in Socrates of Athens. Socrates reminded his contemporaries-in-analysis that a total absence of truth cannot declare itself, and that the quest for truth, however uncertain, includes a certainty about the conditions which make possible the uncertainty. The Socratic irony is a knowing doubt, hence a minimal announcement of some truth. This *docta ignorantia* is a thread running without break through the weave of our tradition. Essays such as the ones gathered in this volume testify to the Socratic legacy.

In our day it is apparent that the question of truth arises, in the present stage of discussion, from two quite different kinds of concern. The one may be called scientific, and the other, ethical, as though we were to say that the one is concerned most of all with "things," the other with "persons." When we follow out the scientific clarification of what we mean by truth, we are very likely to find ourselves in these days in the midst of careful analysis of languages and of scientific methods. Here our leading concern is with linguistic truth. On the other hand, when we follow the ethical concern for truth to the end, we swing the focus of our attention back upon human personality and its veracities. This concern with the veracious and authentic elements of the human situation, now often called "existentialist," deals with existential truth. Whereas the former, linguistic truth, is a truth of propositions, the latter is a truth of commitments. Let us give a moment's thought to each of these concerns, and to their complementary relation to each other.

The intellectual life of our time is being invigorated by a new acumen in treating of linguistic truth. The brilliance of recent linguistic analysis derives from the great renaissance of logic which is still in full swing. Scientific language is nowadays analyzed with a clarity not achieved before. A widespread familiarity with the elements of this analysis can more and more be counted on. By common consent we take a body of scientific knowledge to be a complex structure of sentences, or propositions. The sentences which we accept as assertions are intended to accord with some objective states of affairs. In the interest of objectivity, we focus our attention on the truthfulness of the linkage between the sentences and the objects to which they refer. We abstract as completely as possible from the moods and personal traits of the scientists who utter and test these sentences; though we do not deny, of course, that it is owing to a community and tradition of scientifically trained people that the sentence-clusters called "science" exist at all.

The ideal of scientific objectivity, conceived as linguistic truth, draws us almost irresistibly to the attempt to be objective about human beings, as well as about all the nonhuman things of nature. The goal of a rigorous "behavioristics" (as some call a comprehensive science of man) would be a dispassionate body of linguistic truth about linguists as "behaving" objects.

As the elaboration of "linguistic truth" proceeds, something within us stirs uneasily. The objectivity of the scientific concern obligates us to a sort of official silence about that most inward principle in us which is simply not an object at all, but radically a subject. The conviction gains a hold upon us that there would be no such domain as that endless web of scientific, poetic, and other languages if there were not the inwardness of personal existence from which pours the impulse to speech. How can this conviction claim its own truth? In a negative way, by protesting the claims of impersonal truths about persons. In a positive, and more difficult way, by making articulate an account of the cosmos of inwardness.

The negative way is too easy. It is an oversimplification, for instance, to compare the impersonal aspect of science with the impersonal aspects of the industrial society in which the greater part of our life is immersed, and to deplore both in the same breath. The two things have quite different roots. The former is an achievement of self-forgetful concentration upon truths about nature. The latter are deplorable to the extent that they exhibit crude power of men over men. Surely much of the exploitation and false feeling which disfigure this epoch stem from our easy tolerance of treating persons as things (numbers, units, interchangeable parts). But, by contrast, the selflessness of the scientific calling does silent honor to personal existence. Let this not be forgotten. One tends to forget that about which one is officially silent. And science, regarded from the point of view of "linguistic truth," is officially silent about its underlying personal basis.

The positive case for existential truth can be drawn from the presuppositions of linguistic truth itself. Fortunately the rhythm of experience sees that this is done. When one part of experience is declared to be the whole basis of truth, the neglected part, simply by its presence, builds up an exigency that urges us toward the truer whole. When the impersonal point of view has been perfected to an extreme of precision, there comes the return swing to a reaffirmation of the personal. Or, to put it another way, as the power of scientific objectivity is perfected, the complementary subjectivity of persons becomes intensely apparent by contrast. This is the clue to the varied emphases today on truth in its subjective, ethical aspect, in the form of existential truth. These are the urgent reminders that, as human individuals, we live in the moral medium of history, the dimension of our freedom and deeds. Persons are in their element in history as birds are in their element in the air. In this milieu we are "situated," at once freely and without escape, committed to working out lives possessed of some measure of authenticity.

The reader who bears in mind these two polar aspects of the modern consciousness of truth while he reads the ensuing essays will find himself on familiar ground. Let three anticipations suffice here.

The reader may be impressed with the note of caution that is struck in some of the essays. Truth, in the sense of certitude of knowledge, we are asked to forgo. The search for knowledge cannot be expected to issue in certainties. The scientific methods of inductive procedure yield probabilities, and these are the best we have. These methods of piecemeal advance are suited to the incurable finitude of human intelligence. Probability takes the place of certitude. Here we recognize the focus on scientific, or linguistic, truth.

In the second place, one finds the essays avowing an artistic element in the venture of truth-finding. A natural scientist may properly rely on imagination, or even on the irrationality of "dream," to suggest ways to new scientific discoveries, which are then soberly and methodically ratified by the scientific community. The historian is rightfully guided through his wealth of factual detail by an aesthetic sense for the style of the epoch he is undertaking to interpret. Poetic symbol, creative imagination, sense of style, suggest a shift from linguistic truth simply, with its univocal clarity, toward existential truth. At all events, the appeal is to human creativity.

Finally, one is here reminded of the ethical commitment which operates in the search for truth. Where there is commitment, there is passion—the warrant of serious purpose. Scientific devotion to selfless objectivity draws on a tacit passion. The initiation into a community of language, the language of scientific objectivity, for instance, involves participation in a common commitment. So, also, with entry into the language of religious belief. Certain languages are "convictional" in explicit fashion. All languages are implicitly convictional. The question is raised: "Is there not this ethical presupposition in every shared search for truth?"

It might not be too much to hope that a group of essays which raises the question of truth might at the same time help to lead us to a clearer view of an education in the liberal arts than now prevails. The hope is historically justified. Liberal arts, or liberal disciplines, as we can read in Plato's *Republic,* or in St. Augustine's *De Ordine,* were thought of once as training in the disinterested search for truth, in contrast to vocational training. Indeed, in the majestic pedagogy of antiquity, the ascending scale of liberal arts, commencing with the standards of the right use of language, and proceeding through the exact sciences of nature, led by measured degrees finally to the science of first principles, the central (and divine) truths of the whole system of truth. Modern conceptions of the liberal arts are far, indeed, from any such vision of reasonable order!

Nevertheless, these essays do throw light on several aspects of the inherited meaning of the liberal arts. For one thing, they represent an open dialogue. The quality of disinterested inquiry is apparent throughout, free from the impatience of a vocational demand for "results."

A sort of humanism runs through the discussion also. Whatever truth may be, it is the concern of the totally dedicated artist as a man of integrity; it is the concern of the responsible scientist abiding by the verdict of his fellow scientists in the republic of research; it is the bond of a community of shared religious conviction. The human focus is nowhere hidden for long.

As evidence of the present stage of thinking, the papers testify to the sense of freedom that is implicit in the idea of the liberal arts. Freedom, more than order, is the mark of the present stage of this discussion. Perhaps impatience with the threat of prematurely formulated order is there too, the warning to be on guard against "dogma" in the sense of the unreflective, unexamined affirmation.

The ancient balance of freedom and order in the liberal arts is still to be looked for and worked for. The discussion running through these essays, marked by the qualities of open dialogue, humanism, and freedom, may be the best promise we could wish of an uncoerced recovery of order.

Scientific Truth and the Scientific Method

J. H. Goldstein

INTRODUCTION

This lecture is one of a series which will demonstrate certain differences (and similarities) in emphasis, content, and outlook in a number of the disciplines that make up the modern intellectual kaleidoscope. As the only presentation concerned with modern natural science, this introduction attempts to state, in part by examples, certain salient differences between science and nonscience. The central theme of this paper is the link between scientific method and scientific truth as they are generally interpreted today.

To a scientist one of the strikingly distinctive features of an interdisciplinary nonscientific confrontation is the variety of viewpoints that it can exhibit—and fail to harmonize in the face of conflict and paradox. Even within a given discipline genuinely deep-seated differences are rarely resolved.

In such disputes procedures have seldom been devised which are agreeable to all or nearly all concerned and capable of providing solutions intellectually convincing to the disputants. The debate in sixteenth-century Spain over whether the American Indian conformed to Aristotle's definition of a natural slave, for all its elaborate legalisms and classical scholarship, probably carried little weight with the natives whose despoliation was thus legitimized.[1] More recently, the controversy provoked by the award of the Bollinger Prize in poetry to Ezra Pound,[2] did not apparently lead to

[1] Lewis Hanke, *Aristotle and the American Indians* (Chicago: Henry Regnery Co., 1959).

[2] Archibald MacLeish, *Poetry and Opinion* (Urbana: University of Illinois Press, 1950); Charles Norman, *The Case of Ezra Pound* (New York: Motley Press, 1948).

9

any widespread agreement on the basic points at issue. Not the least of these points was the intriguing question as to whether a work of art could be considered great if it expressed a moral or ethical position incompatible with the prevalent (and traditional) views.

It is true that a great many questions can be subjected to inconclusive discussion, without accompanying overtones like those in the cases cited. Under appropriate circumstances one may fairly expect from such treatments a measure of intellectual stimulation, sharpening of the imagination, and other products of applying scholarship, wisdom, and tolerance to difficult problems, large or small, in art, literature, history, philosophy, and politics.

From the intellectual standpoint, however, what is of especial interest to a scientist is the indecisive character of such discussions. He is, as a rule, disturbed by the infrequency with which agreement is reached, and even more concerned by the apparent absence of any sustained effort to find bases for agreement. Generally unimpressed by the mere magnitude of a question if it provokes only chronically futile disagreement, he prefers to constrict the scope of a question successively until he and his fellows—who are, after all, mere mortals—can cope with it successively and find an acceptable answer. He then enlarges his outlook by linking answer to answer, question to question, so that he is not only unifying the whole but also suggesting more extended and more ambitious questions.

The conscious acceptance of intellectual limitations constitutes a significant difference between the scientific and the humanistic disciplines. It is predicated upon the necessity, implicit in all scientific work, for obtaining general (though not necessarily unanimous) agreement. This contrasts, again, with the nonscientific approach, which tolerates and even encourages diversity when it is competently argued and developed.

The procedure by which scientists obtain, or attempt to obtain, conclusions and propositions that can be generally agreed upon is known as the *scientific method*. The body of observations and generalizations, together with the relevant commentary and interpretations, which have received the assent of the community of scientific workers at any given time is considered *scientific truth*. Scientific truth depends upon scientific methodology.

SOME CHARACTERISTICS OF SCIENTIFIC METHODOLOGY

The general aspects of the scientific method, that is, those procedural features common to the natural sciences, have been widely discussed and have received fairly universal agreement among scientists.[3] There are three points to be considered here:

(1) Scientific work is a social activity. The scientist is dependent upon his predecessors and contemporaries for material and ideas beyond the power of the individual to amass. Even more important, he must submit his work to the scrutiny of the entire scientific community. His results must be acceptable to his colleagues, no matter what their political, racial, or religious orientation, and he cannot dispose of serious arguments by appeals to authority or prestige, or by literary devices. This does not mean that every new idea gains quick and easy acceptance when merited. However, the historical development has shown that the process of open discussion, free of compulsion, has provided the surest and fastest means yet devised for ascertaining the validity of new work.

The importance of such social interaction can scarcely be overemphasized, since no man is infallible. It demands the most serious attention to the problems of clarity and meaning in the communication of ideas and facts. No one who isolates himself in a library can produce what we would call "scientific" work. Certain scholarly fields given to widespread complaint at the alleged entry of scientific procedures into their domain have developed hardly a semblance of this type of interaction. Few, if any, political or religious disputes have even been subjected to this type of discussion, and one can imagine what the consequences of such an approach might have been.

(2) New experience is approached and assimilated through the "hypothetico-deductive" approach. This means that explanatory concepts and ideas are offered tentatively; if they are in accord with the original situation, further consequences are generated by the procedures of deductive logic and subjected to the test of experience.

[3] Philipp Frank, *Philosophy of Science* (Englewood Cliffs, N. J.: Prentice-Hall, Inc., 1957); *The Validation of Scientific Theories* (Boston: Beacon Press, 1956).

The outcome of such tests may be rejection, modification, or retention. Regardless of its status at a given time, no law or theory can be logically considered as final; new experience may at any time indicate the need for change.

Again, this procedure implicitly recognizes the finitude of man's mentality, suggesting that the realms of experience and ideas are creatively linked. It also implies a rejection of the notion of some historical golden age of omniscience, lost but worthy of being regained.

(3) Scientific development occurs in stepwise fashion. This means that scientists tend to approach their problems one at a time, essentially as they appear in the historical evolution of a subject. Naturally, some advances will appear to be quite monumental, as in the case of Quantum Theory, while others may be obviously trivial. Nevertheless, the entire movement of ideas is distinctly different in its nature from that of a philosophical or a religious system dealing with ultimate causes and asserting universal jurisdiction.

The scientific system of knowledge is, therefore, never complete but rather in a perpetual state of dynamic evolution. The development may be termed progressive in the important sense that the area of human experience susceptible to scientific treatment has become steadily larger, richer, and more varied. Whereas half a century ago it was impossible to demonstrate a convincing link between the two basic physical sciences of physics and chemistry, today the line of demarcation has been erased by the application of quantum physics to the problems of chemical binding. Currently, both of these disciplines are penetrating deeply into the life sciences. Indeed, it has often been asserted by proponents of the scientific method that they recognize no prior limits to its applicability.

Experiment and Theory

The hypothetico-deductive approach would be little more than an exercise in logic without the modern version of trial by fire, experimentation (including scientific observation), by means of which the scientist obtains the verdict of experience.

In a scientific experiment one attempts to determine the response of a system (defined in a very general way) to changes of the specified variables which determine the state of the system. The measurements and observations are to be conducted in such a way that the system is unequivocally defined and the variables are under the control of the experimenter, otherwise repetition of the identical experiment by others would be difficult, if not impossible.

Experimentation is, however, indissolubly linked with scientific theory. The latter provides the framework within which any experiment must be formulated; that is, the terms, concepts, and principles used in defining systems and their descriptive variables. Conversely, scientific theories cannot progress very far in advance of the empirical situation without taking on an aspect of speculation. The consequences of this should be well understood: a scientific theory may well propose a radical break with previous conceptions provided that it contains within it the potential for denial as well as affirmation. This requirement insures that a theoretical construction will be related to a sufficiently clear set of referents to permit reasonably decisive experimental tests to be carried out.

THE PROBLEM OF VALIDATION

Scientific validation is not testing theories in routine fashion, albeit with highly precise, costly, or complex instrumentation. It is rather the profoundly different task of harmonizing the theoretical and empirical phases in the structure of a science. A novel theory may require not only a drastic modification in the design of experiments, but also a reorientation in the thought patterns of the experimentalist. The advent of special relativity and quantum theory required a thorough reassessment of the very language of the physical sciences and concurrently refashioned their experimental component along hitherto unimaginable lines.

On the whole, validation is a complex and subtle affair, not to be treated by terse statements of criteria and procedures. Theories involve translation from the world of experience, suitably generalized and abstracted, to a symbolic formalism, which may be mathematical, pictorial, or even verbal. At one point or another, problems of selecting and approximating the central elements of the empirical situation will be encountered, not to mention logical, computational, and linguistic difficulties. It is therefore not surprising that theories or certain phases of theories may be logically correct and empirically false, or conversely. A good part of the daily business of physical science deals with the readjustments and refinements of the detailed situation without undermining the so-called basic principles or fundamentals.

The mechanics and criteria of validation vary considerably. The evaluation of evidence, whether obtained by measurement or classification, appears at times to be somewhat subjective. Despite the importance of measurement and "precision," the lay emphasis on these factors is in a sense misguided and unfortunate. In science the word "precision" is a measure of the reproducibility of measurements or observations, but it is not a guarantee of accuracy or of relevance. Systematic errors are not avoided by high precision. The probable error inferred by the methods of statistics from the most precise clusters of observations has no absolute significance. It must be compared with some other quantity, and this involves matters of judgment.

Granted that we have obtained, under certain criteria, the most reliable answer to a problem, the matter does not end here. It is now necessary to consider the contextual situation: does this result conform with what is already known in a wide field of inquiry? The connections may have to be made indirectly and tortuously, but every new confirmation or failure carries significance. If the validity of a special result can be shown to extend farther and farther afield, often through surprisingly imaginative routes, the general feeling of reliance grows correspondingly. In this fashion the most novel idea or result begins to carry an aura of intuitive acceptability. (In a more slipshod fashion, much the same procedure holds for everyday affairs.)

In general, a certain reserve is exhibited toward results which show little or no connectivity with a wide range of experience. The attitude in such cases probably veers toward suspended judgment rather than dogmatic denial. Although everyone is free to express his opinion on these matters, opinions are not accorded the status of valid scientific results unless they are substantiated along the lines indicated above.

THE SIGNIFICANCE OF MODERN SCIENCE AND ITS ACCOMPLISHMENTS

To grasp properly the full meaning of modern science some knowledge of its intellectual successes and its consequences for other disciplines is necessary, in addition to a familiarity with scientific methodology.

We have, perhaps, grown so accustomed to the panorama of scientific knowledge that we fail to grasp fully the magnificence of its scope as well as the extent to which it overshadows all prescientific efforts to comprehend the universe and man's position in it. The domain of modern science ranges from the nuclear microcosm to the very borders of the universe. The chronologies of species, planets, and galaxies have been charted over almost incomprehensible spans of time. The borderline between living and inert matter has been virtually eliminated and the very origin of life is the subject of much current investigation.[4] Moreover, a survey of the present status of twentieth-century science suggests that we may well be entering an era of intellectual adventures even more remarkable than any yet experienced. In the opinion of many observers, there are no compelling reasons why the general procedures which led to such accomplishments as those listed above cannot be extended to the realm of the everyday affairs of mankind.[5]

One of the hallmarks of scientific methodology is, therefore, *success;* the problems which the scientist sets out to solve have almost invariably succumbed. Moreover, it simply will not do to depreciate scientific accomplishments, for all too many of them represent the answers to once great questions that were not resolved by the rational or intuitive methods of the prescientific age.

It is from the intellectual successes of the special sciences and their impact upon industrial technology (which will not be discussed here) that most of the general consequences of science have been derived. Historians of science have shown that complete autonomy of science has never existed. There have always been links,

---

[4] Albert Ducrocq, *The Origins of Life* (London: Elek Books, 1957).
[5] John Lear, "Peace: Science's Next Great Exploration," *Saturday Review,* XLIII (December 10, 1960), pp. 51-52.

even if implicit, with the prevailing religious, cultural, and philosophical stream and the interaction has been, in varying degrees, a reciprocal one. Often, when a scientific advance has threatened to undermine the foundations of a prior philosophical position, this has been accompanied to some extent by confusion and agitation over the extra-scientific implications of the situation. Generally speaking, the successful consolidation of the scientific position in such cases (e.g., Darwinian evolution) seems to have materially weakened the case for any doctrine in opposition. Certain modern philosophical systems represent, according to some interpreters, a conscious and more or less thoroughgoing effort at adaptation to scientific methodology and its successes. However, since the scientific method seems to have received a more nearly universal acceptance than any philosophical scheme extant, it may be concluded that no unique relationship presently exists between the scientific outlook and any given philosophical system.

The scientist will often be influenced by philosophical considerations (or aesthetic, religious, political, and so on), perhaps unconsciously, but these factors are neither specific nor determinative as regards the ultimate scientific acceptability of his work. On the other hand scientific results may conceivably place a nonscientific discipline in a critical position, requiring either concession, adaptation, or rationalization.

To put the matter in somewhat different terms, any doctrine more general than the body of scientific laws will either lead to testable statements or it will not. If the former, it should be possible, in principle, to examine the validity of the doctrine by (scientifically) testing its consequences. If the latter, then, according to one view (positivism) the doctrine is itself empty.

Whatever attitude one takes toward such analyses, it seems evident that the method and accomplishments of science have left a very deep impression on the intellectual situation of the Twentieth Century.

CONCLUDING REMARKS

We have surveyed some aspects of modern science; specifically, its methods, specialized accomplishments, and general consequences.

All three aspects appear to be very closely related, since it is difficult to imagine that society would long acquiesce in the existence and continued growth of a scientific venture not both successful and relevant to its purposes. Nevertheless, the central feature of science is its method, for this distinguishes science from the other intellectual disciplines.

The contemporary existentialist philosopher, Karl Jaspers, regards the emergence of the scientific method as possibly the most important historical event of the last 2,500 years.[6] Outside scientific circles, however, it would probably be difficult to obtain overwhelming assent to such an evaluation. On the contrary, there appears to be a tendency on the part of many nonscientists to regard the scientific method as severely limited and to resist its introduction into their disciplines. It is no longer novel to hear that the woes of this or that subject can be attributed to the unwarranted intrusion of "the methods of the physical sciences," but it is at times disconcerting to learn that the preferred alternative is a species of rationalism whose previous record of failure is clear.

Why do so many intellectuals view the methods and results of modern science with something akin to uneasiness and distrust? Another contemporary philosopher, Charles Frankel, very pointedly traces such reactions to the failure to distinguish between the individual scientist and science as a social institution.[7] The distinction is crucial, for, as we have remarked earlier, scientific truth can only be established in the public domain. In Frankel's view, the confusion on this point is responsible for our failure to assimilate science effectively, and has had serious practical consequences in the social sphere.

Most scientists would, in my opinion, agree with the position taken by Frankel. Scientists are, in the main, acutely aware of the intellectual hazard created by the aberrations and predispositions of the individual. Science as a social institution, however, provides an effective means for transcending personal intellectual limitations through the process of free and open exchange of ideas and view-

[6] Karl Jaspers, *Reason and Anti-Reason in Our Time* (London: SCM Press, 1952), p. 30.
[7] Charles Frankel. *The Case for Modern Man* (Boston: Beacon Press, 1959), pp. 138-45.

points, and through the continued application of empirical criteria.

In the realm of science, truth is partly the product of a consciously evolved and public, rather than private, procedure. It is also the product of a constant and sometimes extremely difficult individual effort in response to this procedure. As long as the requirements for convincing validation are upheld, this approach tolerates wide individual variation among scientists. The attitudes, beliefs, and temperament of the individual scientist may be of the utmost importance in determining the special interests and the effectiveness of a scientist, but they do not determine the scientific acceptability—the truth content—of his work. The unique power of the scientific method may well rest upon this circumstance.

Suggested Readings

Holton, Gerald, *Introduction to Concepts and Theories in Physical Science.* Cambridge, Mass.: Addison-Wesley, 1952.

von Mises, Richard, *Positivism, A Study in Human Understanding.* Cambridge, Mass.: Harvard University Press, 1951.

Wilson, E. B., Jr., *An Introduction to Scientific Research.* New York: McGraw-Hill Book Company, Inc., 1952.

Hall, A. R., *The Scientific Revolution, 1500-1800.* London: Longmans, Green & Company, 1954.

Feigl, Herbert, and Grover Maxwell, eds., *Current Issues in the Philosophy of Science.* New York: Holt, Rinehart, and Winston, 1961.

Reichenbach, Hans, *The Rise of Scientific Philosophy.* Berkeley: University of California Press, 1951.

Otto, Max, *Science and the Moral Life.* New York: New American Library, 1949.

Barber, Bernard, *Science and the Social Order.* Glencoe, Ill.: The Free Press, 1952.

Truth in the Social
Sciences

Helmut Schoeck

To philosophers and theologians, the word "truth" may seem less pretentious than to the social scientist. Were it not for the challenge of an interdisciplinary setting, the social scientist would hardly be willing to talk about "truth." The best we can do, he is likely to say, is scan the horizon for probabilities, the higher the better, but never more. However, in this essay the traditional *general* meaning of truth, beyond the province of the social or behavioral sciences, is taken for granted.

Establishing truth in the areas of discourse conventionally of interest to the social sciences resembles establishing truth in the courtroom: it is subject to the adversary system. This means that hardly any piece of evidence can be introduced which does not have its waiting adversary. In courts of law, the admissibility and quality of evidence is ruled upon by a presiding judge who instructs the jury what to consider and what to forget. Unfortunately, this kind of judge, imperfect as he may be, is not generally available when social scientists debate. Worse still, unlike the natural scientists, they often have to rely on rather elusive witnesses.

The basic problem of truth today in the social sciences seems to be centered on the relative weight, the quality, the admissibility, and, of course, the comparability of evidence. This is where anarchy prevails. Given a certain public climate, evidence consisting of several psychoanalytical case histories seems acceptable to all, or nearly all; the next moment the same judges will scoff at evidence based on samples of 15,000 respondents. It all depends on whose ox is gored.

Much of the "truth" in the natural sciences depends on the ease with which replication of experiments is possible. But in social science as in the courtroom, the more significant the events we are interested in, the less we can reproduce them. We may be able to reenact small group behavior, but we cannot repeat for tests what twelve men did during a plane crash, nor can we reenact at will a nationwide economic depression. The ultimate test of any scientific attempt to touch, penetrate, and integrate parts of what we take to be reality comes with confirmable (and preferably repeatable) observation of an instance in which mind bends matter or the course of events in the physical universe from what they would have been without human intervention. Until a few years ago one could point to astronomy as an exception. Here, a genuine test of theories and propositions seemed beyond human power. This has changed with man's move into space. Experiment, test, and observation are steps in obtaining a correct, and therefore empowering, understanding of the true state of things.

The social or behavioral sciences have always been restrained by the ethical and psychological limits to experimentations on their subjects. We have to wait for natural occurrences; a nation where minorities are segregated and another where they are (or have been) integrated, for instance. Political reality does not permit setting up for testing purposes on a long-term basis segregated and integrated groups just for observation. We might get volunteers for very limited experiments, say, prisoners, conscientious objectors, or graduate students. But crucial experiments, the kind of gamble on which a natural scientist can stake everything—the effect of the first atomic explosion, for example—are obviously impossible, because of our political and social environment. We cannot even wire a jury room for a tape recorder, as small-group researchers for the University of Chicago Law School found out in the mid-fifties during a national uproar of indignation.

Even a dictatorship, a totalitarian government and its scientists, presumably free from ethical constraints and public opinion, could not bring the behavioral sciences completely into the experimental fields, because before long their subjects would react to and vitiate the experiment—as individuals capable of resentment and indignation. This may be one reason why even the better known social experiments of totalitarian regimes—Soviet Russia's tampering with the basic family unit in the Twenties, Red China's scheme along similar lines with the communes in 1958, Hitler's attempt to get a scientifically mated population—have been few, brief, and vain. One could argue that absolute governments usually have less freedom to let social science (no matter how perverted) experiment than less autocratic systems, since they need all their time and energy to stay in power. Apparently they can do this best when they leave untouched as much of ordinary interpersonal relations as possible. Machiavelli's advice to the Prince still seems valid: you can do anything to and with your subjects as long as you leave their religion and women alone. If we extend the two items a little we see much of social relations covered by Machiavelli's warning.

Being more limited than the natural scientists in setting up reality for a test—except in areas where our observations may be trivial and for that reason may tolerate genuine experiment—we do have, of course, various criteria for selecting data likely to yield a correct picture of reality. Again, some of them are quite elementary and were probably used in court before scholarship adopted them. For instance, the *forensic* nature of the quest for truth, or, at any rate, for the highest attainable probability is quite obvious in the following procedure. The historian, political scientist, or sociologist can usually claim greater veracity for his findings if he can show that somewhere along the line of generating those data, someone was responsible for them who had a generally known, or frankly admitted, bias against the direction of the final data. Today's economists may cite Karl Marx with a statement about the immense productivity of the capitalistic economic system, because Karl Marx can be presumed to have given this praise only grudgingly, and on the basis of evidence which, even to him, seemed overwhelming. Or, if a historian finds an account of an event or conversation favorable to a dynasty in an opposition newspaper, he will often prefer this source as of self-evident strength.

In any case, much more of our solid knowledge than many social scientists care to admit depends on the reliability of the historian's work. Max Weber, by almost universal consent a giant of modern sociology, obtained most of his raw data from historians (significantly, his own training in history, languages, and jurisprudence enabled him to do this more judiciously and critically than his contemporary Vilfredo Pareto, who had come to sociology from engineering). If modern sociology and anthropology were suddenly to doubt the capability of historians to produce "truth," those disciplines might find themselves in a vacuum. For instance, in doing research on a problem of social stratification we usually insist on knowing who came first to a place, how, from where, what images of his own past he brought to the new community, and so on. All these facts, at least until very recently, had to be learned from the historian.

Whatever we call truth in the sciences is a stage of a process. This process goes on partly under its own momentum, independent of human interference (e.g., a vanishing lake may reveal a lost ancient city), but it can also move like a levee-controlled river— channeled into more specific paths so that it will become more visible. Although most of us act as if "truth" were ultimately possible, we content ourselves with degrees of probability and plausibility. But hardly any researcher can convince his fellows of the probability and plausibility of his findings and underlying or derived theories unless he commands a certain credibility. To get it he commits himself to a method or sets of methods. But in the interplay of these concepts and attitudes, specific dangers lurk for anyone who employs improper procedures while neglecting, for what he believes to be scientific reasons, other methods and conceptualizations which would be helpful to him in his search for truth about social man. There are many methods but only one proper attitude about their use.

It is often fruitful to focus on threats to truth before saying too much about truth itself. We can assume a general understanding of what we mean by seeking reasonably accurate information about the dimensions of reality in which men conduct and experience their social affairs. Aside from elementary errors, common to all fields of systematic knowledge, we encounter a few hindrances to "truth" which are endemic in the behavioral sciences. Quite often we permit a method, which is favored for its halo effect, to determine and restrict to its own province the ways in which correct knowledge is sought. One might even argue, and cite impressive cases from the history of science, that the social sciences have diminished their chances for dramatic breakthroughs to novel knowledge (although the subject matter itself may not permit "break-throughs") because of a compulsiveness about proper methodology due to a misunderstanding of what is going on in the natural sciences. The creative and successful researcher in the natural sciences often appears more relaxed and flexible in his selection of method or methods than the social scientist.

The late Howard Becker, in a public lecture in 1959, cited pejorative epithets of which the sociologist today has become so fearful that he may even run away from a good problem and a possible approach to it lest he be labeled, for instance, "armchair scholar." We all know this cliché. It seems to imply that vigorous moving around for first-hand collecting of some sort of data ("legwork") is intrinsic to scientific work. But are the masters of the microscope, conventional or electronic, mere armchair scientists? Is there a basic difference between the anatomist, geologist, or geneticist, sitting behind his microscope, looking at specimens, and the economist or demographer sitting in a library poring over long columns of printed data from various sources? Obviously a man with an immense memory for forms, color shades, textures, and so forth, could become a creative discoverer behind his microscope even though he never quite learned how to obtain specimens, freeze and cut them to proper thinness, and dye them. He will have learned these skills in his career before delegating the task. But in many instances, especially when making a comparative study based on slides sent him by colleagues from other parts of the world, he will train his mental powers and memory on finished data supplied to him, without striking us as an armchair scholar. Why? Is it because the social scientist is expected to come face-to-face with his subject matter, men, whereas the microscopist actually looks at concrete bits of reality?

Yet neither the social scientist using census data, especially when he uses them from many periods and various countries, nor the natural scientist, can be expected as a matter of economy to have collected all these primary data personally before being allowed to retreat to his study. What distinguishes all these researchers from an amateur or layman is that they are expected to have the peripheral knowledge and some personal experience in order to judge the reliability of what they find under the microscope or in the printed data. The anatomist must know that tissue obtained from a particular location in the body is more likely to have artifacts than tissues obtained from other parts. The demographer ought to know that the data obtained from, or for, a certain population group or geographic area are less reliable than those from elsewhere.

The time element in truth has much greater implications for social science than for other fields. Large sections of our subject matter (populations, birth rates, migrations, forms of government) constantly undergo "social change" (often completely against the best available predictions; see the failure to predict the rapid population growth in the United States since 1940). In addition to, and often intertwined with, social change *per se,* the notions of what is worthwhile and desirable "truth" in the social sciences changes. Social scientists have not yet agreed on the constancy or nature of human nature. Clyde Kluckhohn once suggested that the earliest and basic human experience—the first months and years within the nuclear family, for biological reasons, are so similar that, with psychoanalytical theories to back us, we can assume some universal elements in human personality and social structure. This seems tenable.

As pointed out earlier, "truth" for the most part is a location of emphasis in a field of generally known facts or phenomena. The social scientist infrequently discovers something the layman has not noticed long ago, but the social scientist claims a mandate and special competence in placing relative weight on the phenomenon. We might cite the late Ralph Linton, and others, who thought that perhaps the most significant "truth" social science uncovered in the first half of the twentieth century was the full recognition of what the concept "culture" implies in modern anthropology. Often a social scientist's fame consists of coining or preempting a concept. Hundreds of authors over the centuries have pointed to a human tendency which David Riesman in 1950 emphasized as "other-directedness."

When asked to talk about "truth" in his field the social scientist often feels hesitant because by the time he has rephrased his discovery in ordinary language for the inquiring layman, the thing itself has become quite ordinary. It is the importance, the weight given to this particular phenomenon—recorded through a concept —that interests the social scientist.

In almost any of the natural sciences the student, if asked by a layman "what truths have you people discovered lately?" can name at least half a dozen major substantive accomplishments for the past twenty years. The student in the social sciences finds it difficult to match this feat. He may reel off a few names of great men in his discipline—but soon he will stop and realize that they have merely introduced new concepts, or an aptly phrased theory, but their fame rarely rests on a decisive new approach to reality. He might think of one or the other major classifier, systematizer in his field—a man who placed all tribes of an area into some kind of order—but again, is this truth? When we look around for better known empiricists in our field, we hesitate to cite their accomplishments to our inquiring friend. If he is fairly alert and wise to the world, he already suspects it to be true that more people find sex fun than admit it, that lower-class students usually do not get so far in education as middle-class students, and that lower-class people cannot speak the language of a psychoanalyst and consequently derive little benefit from psychiatry. Somehow all this sounds less thrilling and compelling than truth-seeking in the nonsocial sciences. Why? One answer comes to mind: the trouble with the social scientist is that he cannot see beauty, aesthetic coherence, in the *what is*. At best he can hope for beauty in a utopia that he has yet to help bring about. The physicist pushes toward what he hopes to be the thing itself. The core of matter can be a haven for his mind. The student of social man usually applies himself to interpersonal phenomena he fervently hopes will have vanished before he has completed his work.

The natural scientist from the very beginning set out to explore a realm of intrinsic beauty and apparently coherent structure. Aristotle urged his students to recognize the beauty even in a cadaver. Johann Kepler (1571-1630) declared it to be the task of the astronomer simply to rethink (and perhaps map for all time), without intervening, the beauty of the Creator's thought underlying the universe. In contrast, today hardly any social scientist will admit beauty or aesthetic sense in what he studies. He knows that the ways of the exotic people are far from what Rousseau thought they were. And in any case we worry so much about the poor diet of an isolated tribe that we have no time to admire the inherent beauty of a ritual or custom. A researcher may be charmed by the beauty of a sudden social action, such as a revolution that "came off beautifully," but unless hopelessly committed to perpetual revolution he rarely finds anything to admire in the aftermath of the revolutionary act. The functional school in sociology, it must be admitted, occasionally does show an aesthetic pleasure in pointing out the stabilizing effect of, let us say, the norm of reciprocity, but for this very reason this school is suspect by some in the profession.

Typically, the social scientist today is unhappy with what he has to study. He is alienated from his subject matter—social interaction as it is found among mankind. Often, the more he discovers the true state of things the more he wishes never to have seen it, because he may have to admit that the order he is after, utopia, may be more distant than he thought. This experience is rare with the natural scientist. He can interlock himself, can grasp a segment of the world very much in the way the earliest scientists did. At least up to the atomic age, the natural scientist seldom felt responsible for what he saw and studied. Discovering a nova or a new bacillus did not bring any new qualms about mankind's collective guilt.

When I find the social scientist to be a man who rarely recognizes beauty in his subject matter, I have in mind not only those who are in search for ugliness. The muckrakers, the students of crime and perversion, of urban decay and international tensions—their preoccupation is related to what I am saying, but the problem goes beyond a mere focusing on the seamy underside of social life. It may be intrinsic to the modern social sciences that, unlike the natural scientist, their practitioners and theories cannot come to grips with any aesthetic dimension in social reality. There have been very few attempts to use concepts such as symmetry and asymmetry in behavioral science research. Of course, prior to about the middle of the nineteenth century students of social affairs occasionally did marvel at the inherent beauty of human institutions. And even some recent sociologists—the analytical school— have approached social reality, in their search for pure forms of social relations, fully aware of aesthetic possibilities. When noting the loss of the aesthetic dimension in social science, I am speaking of the *present* situation.

To recognize, to admit an aesthetic structure in any phenomena, we have to differentiate and accept a hierarchical order in what we see. This the social scientist finds difficult not so much for reasons inherent in his intellectual apparatus, but for reasons connected with the impetus that has driven him to become a social scientist. The contemporary American social scientist usually feels committed to the nonrecognition of functionally valid hierarchy. This bias—or blind spot—has been stressed by the American sociologists, Everett C. Hughes, Kingsley Davis, and Wolfram Eberhard, among others.

However, the problem may lie deeper. First, a certain eccentricity, a marginal or peripheral situation in one's society, may be a prerequisite for the inquiring mind. We have studies showing that the person considered odd, eccentric, self-centered, one who was the only child, and so on, has a better chance of becoming a creative scientist than the individual happily enshrined in a society whose perfection he never has reason to doubt. The physicist or chemist, as well as the sociologist, psychologist, or anthropologist, may have a personal idiosyncrasy, which is concomitant or even prerequisite to the mind of a researcher. A difference between the natural scientist and the student of man, however, begins to emerge and become relevant to the latter's subject matter when we compare the two main fields of natural and social science. No matter how antagonistic or alienated a physicist or astronomer may be from his own society, he will have little reason to close his eyes to the natural structure, the aesthetic coherence in the structure of a solar system, a molecule, or even a chromosome. He does not have to kick the universe for revenge upon a society which failed to enthrone him as a philosopher-king. (He may, of course, as a sideline, become a self-styled expert on world peace and join the ranks of the social scientist on that issue.)

The social scientist has an unhappier lot than his big brother in the natural sciences: his alienation from the existing society, or at least what he perceives to be the existing society and its history, though it may have been a prerequisite for making him a scientist, will find no outlet but the very subject matter he is going to study.

We have to distinguish here between an attitude of detachment, neutrality, objectivity, perhaps, and an attitude of resentment. We would hardly expect a man who hates flowers because his mother always sent him with a bouquet to a much disliked aunt to become a good botanist. But some sociologists have gone as far as to say that a deep, burning resentment of one's society is a prerequisite for becoming a sociologist.[1] Can one understand what one resents? Nearly all our pedagogical and educational experiments have shown the exact opposite to be true.

Edward Shils, a University of Chicago sociologist, published an article a few years ago about the social function in British society of the coronation of Queen Elizabeth II. He showed how such a national event provides a symbolic force even for a modern divergent mass democracy. The beauty of the symbol, and its beneficial function as far as the cohesion and survival of British society and culture is concerned, was the subject and thesis of Shils. For this he was severely taken to task by a young American sociologist holding a permanent position at the London School of Economics, who decried the mortal sin of the social scientist committed by Shils. How could Shils dare to emphasize the aesthetic value and social function of so costly, so reactionary a symbol as a queen's coronation?[2] Inasfar as symbols, except for novel and unproven ones, in every society necessarily represent the past and its commandment to the present and future, it seems that the social scientist in fear of conservative or reactionary predilections cannot deal with the phenomenon of symbol in its aesthetic context without

[1] So, verbatim, George Simpson, *A Sociologist Abroad* (The Hague: Martin Nijhoff, 1959), p. 168. See also Edward Shils: "Professor [C. Wright] Mills implies that sociology has more to gain from a hostile attitude toward the existing order than from uncritical incorporation into it. It is true that, in taking this position, he stands in a distinguished tradition. Nonetheless, neither his viewpoint nor its opposite is correct. Neither the unqualified hatred of the outsider nor the uncritical affirmation of the patriot opens the path to truth about society." "Professor Mills on the Calling of Sociology," *World Politics*, XIII (July 1961), p. 608 n. Reprinted by permission.

[2] Edward Shils and Michael Young, "The Meaning of the Coronation," *The Sociological Review*, I (December 1953), pp. 63-81. N. Birnbaum, "Monarchs and Sociologists," *ibid.*, III (July 1955), pp. 5-23.

admitting a function of something that according to his professed ideology ought not to be.[3]

The situation of the social scientist in the twentieth century is somewhat akin to the situation of the creative artist who also, in the opinion of some literary critics, has developed an exaggerated preoccupation with the ugly side of human life. Indeed, the artist's increasing focus on a caricature of man and his institutions has attracted scholarly demonstration. Jacques Barzun, in his *House of Intellect*,[4] has pointed out the same preoccupation in the social sciences. But the creative artist has one advantage over the social scientist: as far as his method and medium of expression is concerned, he can strive for absolutes, for perfection—indeed, for beauty and truth. No matter what ugly scenes and emotions the poet or novelist may describe, his style, his linguistic structure, may still be artistic in itself. This is true for the other art forms as well. The modern social scientist has no such escape from ugliness and triviality. Tenement houses, abortion and illegitimacy rates, suicide and morbidity rates, mob actions, and most of the other things that occupy him are not any prettier when tabulated and correlated by Univac than by hand.

Moreover, the contemporary behavioral scientist has banished beauty and its aesthetic comprehension from his field partly because, accepting for his own work only a limited range of methods used in the natural sciences, he has closed his eyes, and thus his field, to form. To me this is an unnecessary self-limitation. We even have a name for it, scientism. In order to claim the mantle of pure and rigorous science, many social scientists refuse to recognize as scientific—let alone use—certain approaches to reality which validate through consensus on forms, structures, or *Gestalten*. Anatomy,

[3] Among the few American sociologists who have given attention to this problem is Hugh Dalziel Duncan, *Language and Literature in Society* (Chicago: University of Chicago Press, 1953). See especially the chapters "Symbols and Authority" and "Hierarchy and Symbols in Democratic Society."

See also the controversy between Kingsley Davis and Melvin M. Tumin in the pages of the *American Sociological Review*, XVIII (1953), and Davis and Buckley in XXIII (1958) and XXIV (1959).

[4] Jacques Barzun, *The House of Intellect* (New York: Harper & Brothers, 1959), chapter 1.

hematology, botany, geology, crystallography and other disciplines could not do without admissibility of evidence on which researchers can agree solely through exchange of qualitative, descriptive verbal statements. The late Clyde Kluckhohn, Harvard anthropologist, saw this clearly.[5]

No scientist, social or natural, can expect perpetual public trust in his findings and conclusions simply because he happens to be called "scientist." Some laymen, even more perhaps than scientists, seem to believe that the vocation of science and research in itself imbues its practitioners with greater veracity, candidness, self-criticism, and objectivity than the ordinary human possesses. And yet there are scientists who doubt this assumption. For instance, Anne Roe, of the Graduate School of Education of Harvard University, writing recently on the psychology of the scientist, dismissed the usual characterizations of scientists which "emphasize the objectivity of their work and describe their cold, detached, impassive, unconcerned observation of phenomena which have no emotional meaning for them." For Dr. Roe, this could hardly be further from the truth. She reminds us of many historical instances of errors in science which the author of the idea has never been able to see or admit. Many scientists are essentially unaware of the fact of personal commitment, often living by a "myth of impersonal objectivity."[6]

The more sophisticated layman might think that among scientists and scholars there is some kind of self-policing that makes fraud and self-deception impossible because of the nature and organization of scientific work. This is questionable. We face here a major problem connected with what P. W. Bridgman has called "public versus private scientific proof." Certainly "verification by public report" sometimes helps to define truth. Knowledge is said to be scientific knowledge in the degree to which it is publicly confirmable. As Bridgman emphasizes, this demand can be met in many

[5] Clyde Kluckhohn, "Common Humanity and Diverse Cultures," in *The Human Meaning of the Social Sciences*, ed. by Daniel Lerner (New York: Meridian Books, 1959), pp. 266-70.

[6] Anne Roe, "The Psychology of the Scientist," *Science*, CXXXIV (August 18, 1961), pp. 456-58. Reprinted by permission.

situations of physics. Yet even here we find "special situations in which public observation or confirmation is impossible 'in principle.'" [7] In the final analysis, public acceptance of observations represents only "the consensus of individual physicists, each of whom was individually convinced of the validity of the law by activities essentially private."

Thus, in essense, private (often "classified" or secret) activities of individuals, even though made public in one form or another, constitute the test of "public acceptance" in science. Falling prey to a hoax or conspiracy is not ruled out by the methods and procedures. No scientist in any field, when suspected of distorting the data in reading and interpreting them, is justified in replying with an indignant "But I am a scientist." [8] As Karl R. Popper has pointed out, only one small peculiarity makes the scientist different from the ordinary man: in order to claim the mantle of science, one ordinarily has to use, and make public, records and to limit oneself to kinds of data which lend themselves to replication, duplication, and checking by individuals other than the originator and his immediate staff. The hoax or forgery in science and by scientists is a possibility here as in other fields. The Piltdown forgery is in recent memory, and C. P. Snow's *The Affair* has reminded us of possibilities most academic men would have preferred to keep buried.

The public and fellow scholars are usually at the mercy of "truth by IBM card," on which so much in today's social science depends. From datum or interview schedule to punched card in a complex electronic device is a long way fraught with human and mechanical error. The late Alfred C. Kinsey and his team unloaded on our legal conscience shocking percentages that probably have already had an effect on the judicial and legislative processes. But no one outside the professional students of sex ever had a chance to check the primary data. The "truth" about our society's sex behavior, at final count obtained from some 18,000 interviews, resides in paper

[7] P. W. Bridgman, *The Nature of Physical Knowledge*, ed. by L. W. Friedrich (Milwaukee: The Marquette University Press, 1960), pp. 16 ff.

[8] See C. P. Snow's address, reprinted in *Science*, CXXXIII (January 27, 1961), pp. 256ff.

cards behind jealously guarded combination locks, further protected by a code to which a key existed only in the memory of Dr. Kinsey and his associates.

Actually, the elusive value called truth is hardly better protected in science than in our legal system. In court we have to assume that witnesses and jurors have not been bribed. Much of our accepted knowledge in various fields of scientific endeavor rests on the implicit acceptance of a basic honesty on the part of those who did the work. And yet scientists occasionally do doubt each other's work on such prescientific grounds. For some approaches used in research there are no safeguards against systematic errors which might result from the desire to obtain a certain result. This creates peculiar problems. For instance, Professor Rhine, the leading proponent of research into extra-sensory perception, offers us a case in which "truth" hinges on imputed credibility. In 1955, Dr. George R. Price suggested in an article that the long statistical series published by Professor Rhine indeed would offer mathematically and scientifically acceptable proof for the theory of extra-sensory perception, provided one does not doubt the integrity of Professor Rhine and his associates in recording and processing their data. In view of the controversial nature of extra-sensory perception, Dr. Price continued, it is justifiable to have this doubt concerning the work of Dr. Rhine.[9]

In 1961, Anne Roe voiced the same suspicion: to her all the apparatus of modern science merely extends the range of our sensory and conceptual capacities. Therefore, the information provided by such extensions eventually reaches a form in which we, with our biological limitations, can receive it. Here, errors may slip in. Roe points out that "the direction of the error is more likely than not to be associated with the observer's interest in how the findings come out." And she mentions, as perhaps the clearest case of this kind, research on extra-sensory perception. The disparity in figures on radioactive fallout might also reflect such factors.[10]

[9] George R. Price, "Science and the Supernatural," *Science,* CXXII (August 26, 1955), pp. 359-67.
[10] Anne Roe, *loc. cit.,* p. 456.

With all these systematic doubts I agree. However, a tantalizing question emerges. What if the potential findings of a particular line of research threaten to be so unpopular politically, religiously, or emotionally, that no one except a single researcher and his associates are willing to go through the necessary procedures to research the question? For instance, if none but Dr. Rhine and his students are willing to pursue the possibility of extra-sensory perception, how can they ever be vindicated or refuted?

If we consider science an open-ended procedure with an indefinite life-span, and if we also ignore its historical responsibility to human problems at any given time, we could say that the "scientific court" never completely dismisses an insufficiently aired issue. However, when we set a reasonable time limit for this scientific court to outgrow its temporary bias or blindness—a period of one or two generations—we can show amazing exclusions of evidence and possible research avenues.

Indeed, there is a strong assumption that as a particular field or science in general progresses and becomes more and more institutionalized, the less likely are unorthodox and potentially embarrassing investigations in it. In other words, formerly with less fixed research procedures, and less financial and reputational dependence on institutions and the good will of organized science, the individual researcher could venture into an approach or a field that today would immediately bring upon him the merciless ridicule and threats of his contemporaries and colleagues. (The history of medicine throughout the nineteenth century offers abundant documentation for this.) The more science becomes big business, the more money is at stake and the more the good will of the money sources—private or public—is at stake, the greater the effective pressure for orthodoxy.[11] The more anxiously the social scientist vies for status with the mighty policy makers in his society, and the more he tries to gain assurance by emphasizing the methods of the natural sciences, the more elusive he may find the problem of "truth."

[11] See B. Barber, "Resistance by Scientists to Scientific Discovery," *Science*, CXXXIV (September 1, 1961), pp. 596 ff.

Suggested Readings

Polanyi, Michael, *Personal Knowledge*. Chicago: University of Chicago Press, 1958.

Popper, Karl R., *The Logic of Scientific Discovery*. London: Hutchinson & Company, Ltd., 1959.

Schoeck, Helmut, and James W. Wiggins, eds., *Scientism and Values*. Princeton: D. Van Nostrand Company, Inc., 1960.

Truth in History

Walter D. Love

"Truth in history" is a phrase that raises a bevy of problems, too many of which escape in a rush. Those that seem easy to grasp have a way of wriggling free after a while, and some of them may disintegrate at a touch; but I shall try to hold to two or three of them long enough to describe them and to say what I think of them.

I cannot speak for all historians. For many there are no problems; they simply do their work without wondering whether they can or do deal with truth. Others see problems but refrain—practicably—from dwelling upon them, and accept them as inevitable hazards of the profession. But some historians have done a certain amount of public soul-searching about the problems of truth in history: they worry about whether so-called "objectivity" is possible in history; they wonder whether historical method is "scientific"; and they speculate on whether we can know the ultimate significance, the "meaning" of the whole past. All our journals are invaded by papers of their sort, most of which have been delivered to drowsing banqueteers, for speakers to historical societies are particularly devoted to them. Moreover, historians are constantly called upon to review books on the nature of history written by philosophers, sociologists, anthropologists, or theologians, since the problems of history have aroused a flood of comment from outsiders, particularly in the last few years. It really takes a stubborn and intellectually provincial historian to remain untouched.

There are probably two main reasons for the current worry about truth in history. The first is that for more than a century, all studies have been drastically "historicized." Scholars have tried to explain everything by history. We historicize the physical world in geology and in Darwinian biology. We think of human life as a sequence of institutions, customs, and shared ideas. We have accounts of the "evolution" of the novel and lyric and the "development" of the English house. We even have "histories" of sex. Habitually we think of ourselves or all men—of the whole universe—in time sequence.

The results of historicizing have been disappointing. We assumed that if you tell the history of a thing, you have explained it. Carl Becker once demonstrated this by contrasting modern thinkers with St. Thomas Aquinas, who was strong on philosophical definitions:

> Let St. Thomas ask *us* to define anything [he says]—for example, the natural law—let him ask us to tell him what it *is*. We cannot do it. But, given time enough, we can relate for him its history. We can tell him what varied forms the natural law has assumed up to now. Historical-mindedness is so much a preconception of modern thought that we can identify a particular thing only by pointing to the various things it successively was before it became that particular thing which it will presently cease to be.[1]

This passage need not arouse that peculiar nostalgia which has induced some people to try to embrace St. Thomas and all his works and to fall back into his age. We need not give up our histories of planets and species, parliaments, novels, lyrics, houses, and sex. The moral of Becker's contrast is that the history of something is not its only satisfactory and complete explanation, as so many modern people imagine. By claiming so much for history they have provoked a healthy reaction. The historical approach has been dropping out of one area of study after another—law, religion, theology, political science, sociology, even English—as scholars try supplementary approaches. For instance, Henry Nash Smith once proclaimed in an informal talk that every English department in the country has been split right down the middle, between the low- (or middle-) brows who still study literary compositions historically, trying to understand them by explaining the men who produced them and the "times" in which they were produced, and the high-brows who seek understanding and explanation through symbolism, or through the relation of literary works to religious schemes, or by

---

[1] Carl L. Becker, *The Heavenly City of the Eighteenth-Century Philosophers* (New Haven: Yale University Press, 1952), p. 19. Reprinted by permission.

confining themselves to a kind of internal criticism in which a work is studied simply as a structure. History can hardly be the truth, the whole truth, and nothing but the truth. It seems odd now that anyone could have pretended that it was.

The second reason for the current lively interest in truth in history is that a battery of criticism has been loosed against the methods of doing historical work—by historians themselves, as well as by philosophers, sociologists, and logicians. It has been pointed out, in countless little ways, that while historians hardly attain the *whole* truth, what they do attain is not truth at all, but only probability, opinion, guesswork, prejudice, or even less. The pronouncements have been extreme: "In spite of all his efforts . . . the historian cannot gain an adequate knowledge of what has been." "The world of history is an intangible world, recreated imaginatively, and present [only] in our minds." Writing history is merely "an act of faith." No history is objective and final, because we all must view the past from a certain "perspective"; "every generation must rewrite history for itself." [2] You will recognize these statements as the current crop of platitudes. Many of them have become nearly meaningless through repetition, and much of their effectiveness has been lost now that they are no longer shocking. Their popularity, however, must remind us that not only have people begun to doubt that history yields the whole truth; they have also begun to doubt that history yields truth at all.

I

Let us consider a few of the problems the historical method poses. For the sake of neatness, I would like to consider these few problems in two categories, following the old distinction between "fact" and "interpretation" (or "significance," or "explanation"— whatever words will suggest the opposition between describing "what happened" and the meanings we attach to what happened). This distinction has fallen into disrepute; careless people used to

[2] For many such statements, see the anthology edited by Hans Meyerhoff, *The Philosophy of History in Our Time* (New York: Doubleday and Co., 1959); the quotations are from Henri Pirenne, Carl L. Becker, Charles A. Beard, and John Dewey, pp. 93, 128, 140, 172. Reprinted by permission.

talk as if historical work is always to be neatly divided into two steps: first find the facts, then "interpret" them, tell what they mean. People still more careless imagined that the second step was dictated by the first, when they used the slogan of thirty years or so ago, "We just follow the facts wherever they lead." It had to be pointed out to them that the same set of facts might be used in contrary interpretations, depending upon the contrary assumptions and biases of different historians. It had also to be pointed out that facts themselves are constructions, and are liable to be dependent upon the same assumptions and biases. The first group of problems to face, then, are the problems of what historical facts really are.

To use Carl Becker's definition, facts are "statements" about "events, acts, thoughts, emotions" and these "have forever vanished as actual occurrences." [3] Notice that facts are *only* statements—we never have the events, the happenings, for which the "facts" seem to stand. They are either made by us or handed to us in books, having been made by others. The ambiguity of the word "fact" ought to remind us constantly of the distance between what we *assert* happened in the past and those happenings themselves. To portray the greatness of the distances between our "facts" and the realities they are supposed to assert, one need only notice that the most simple fact is an elaborate construction. Take the hackneyed example, "In the year 49 B.C., Caesar crossed the Rubicon." Becker used it to show that this fact is not even a simple unit, because it is not a reference to some simple event. It is really a "simple generalization of a thousand and one facts" [4]—all those events that add up to Caesar's crossing the Rubicon: thousands of men and horses stumbling through the waters, Caesar fretting, hallooing, and pronouncing ("The die is cast"). Within a "fact," it seems, is a world of more "facts"; or to put it less paradoxically: even the simplest-looking fact may stand for an indeterminate number of actions or events.

Worse still, the fact is supposed to stand for a host of other events outside or beyond an event like the crossing of the Rubicon.

[3] Carl L. Becker, "What Are Historical Facts?" in Meyerhoff, *op. cit.*, p. 125. Reprinted by permission.
[4] *Ibid.*, p. 122. Reprinted by permission.

In common usage we have appropriated this event as a figure of speech for an irrevocable decision, because it stands for Caesar's decision to start the civil wars. Here is a workaday historian of fifty years ago, portraying the fact as a key event in Caesar's whole life and in the context of the series of events that were the civil wars of his time:

> Caesar sent in advance officers (Plut. "Caes.," 32), without any military display, quickly to seize the town of Arminium, thus beginning the civil war, even before he himself crossed the bridge over the little Rubicon. This he accomplished after nightfall, with deliberate privacy, attended only by a small number of men deep in his confidence. Even the dinner company which he had left were not informed of his immediate action. He had driven fast, but when he came to the rivulet he halted; no reason to doubt in the least what seems to have been remembered and recorded by Asinius Pollio: the phrase that rose to his lips, too, from Menander's "Arrephoros," a commonplace of that culture, ending in the words, "Let the die be cast!" escaped him, not pompously nor histrionically, but that agony of the soul, that endless weighing and computing, was now at an end. Resolution unfetters the soul.[5]

This historian has obviously moved from fact into the area of interpretation. And that was one of Becker's points: apparently we never bother to assert or to create a *bare* fact, we seem always to do it in a context where it is to stand for more than an isolated event. Not only is a fact already a kind of generalization, in that it refers to many events; it also comes to us fairly dripping with significance because of the context from which it is torn.

There is another difficulty about facts. Every one of them is a more or less elaborate inference from some evidence. When we picture an event (or, more precisely, some events) that a statement is supposed to evoke, we try to tie the picture to evidence. Becker used the Rubicon fact as an example by plucking it out of his memory. He is almost as sure of it as of anything else he can remember, but he would sense that there is a difference between his memory of this and his memory of his own experiences—for example, a childhood memory of crossing the Mississippi; he knows

[5] E. G. Sihler, *Annals of Caesar* (New York: G. E. Stechert and Company, 1911), pp. 194-195. Copyright 1910 by E. G. Sihler. Reprinted by permission.

that he only makes the Rubicon-crossing *like* a memory by an act of willful imagination. It is a kind of analogizing. He relies on the assumption that other people, on whose knowledge of Caesar's crossing the Rubicon he depends, really had this in *their* memories as past experience, and that they left records. But we have only records of records of records when we reach back so far into the past. There is a whole genealogy of witnesses between him and the actual witnesses. Think of the gigantic structure of inferences that it takes to get from Becker to Caesar's witnesses! And the structure may be full of flaws: witnesses lied, and Caesar never crossed the Rubicon; or he really crossed some other river; the story of Caesar himself is only a myth that got mixed up with authentic history; or perhaps all that has been written about the ancients was made up by fourteenth-century monks. This last was seriously asserted by some of the historical critics of the eighteenth century. I should not be at all surprised to open one of our own historical journals some day to an article entitled, "The Rubicon: Did Caesar Cross It?" In fact, a fairly recent biographer treats the evidence for this "simple fact" with a rather puzzled delicacy. Having followed Caesar from his dinner company to the bank of the river, he complains:

From this time it becomes impossible to follow the exact order of events and to distinguish the true from the false. The ancient authors seem to have taken a particular pleasure in embellishing their accounts of this episode with evocative and not always very well-founded details. Some of them, however, suggest a direct, first-hand observation which cannot be disregarded. Asinius Pollio, the celebrated friend of Horace, Virgil, and Augustus, and one of the few intimates whom Caesar admitted to his confidence, wrote down for posterity his impressions as an eye-witness. But they have reached us through the somewhat free rendering of Plutarch. The chief thing we gather from them is that Caesar seems to have hesitated at the last moment. Appian, who does not mention the source of his information, gives the same impression. He even attributes to Caesar the following words on this occasion: "Friends, if I do not cross this river, my holding back will be the source of my misfortunes; if I do cross it, it will bring misfortune to the whole human race." In order to induce him to advance, Suetonius finds it necessary to introduce at the last moment a miraculous and providential flute-player who, seizing the instrument of one of Caesar's musicians, rushed toward the river sounding the march with all his might and drew from Caesar this final cry which has ever remained fresh in the memory of mankind: "Let us go forward whither the signs of the gods and the injustice of our enemies call us. The die is cast!"

Our biographer is dismayed at the confusion of the evidence, commenting somewhat bitterly, "All this is a little too close to fiction for the historian to accept it without seeking elsewhere for the facts." He proceeds then to construct a fact:

Suetonius also makes a brief reference to the horses which on Caesar's orders were set free as an offering to the god of the River Rubicon in order to make him favorably disposed to the enterprise. This is a point which deserves some attention. It is certain that Caesar himself, whose indifference to religious matters was notorious, had no need to fortify his own decision by a proceeding of this kind. There were, however, the soldiers who were simple uneducated men, animated for the most part by a very real faith. This gesture must indubitably have been made for their benefit and its aim was to get them into the right frame of mind.

"Indubitably" here must warn the reader that the fact created is not at all indubitable, but quite as debatable as any of those written by the embellishing ancients, and no further removed from "fiction." Pleased to have made up his mind about this one little snippet from Suetonius, our biographer rattles on, speculating and extending from his "fact." Caesar's soldiers, he says,

must have been greatly surprised at finding themselves suddenly brought to the banks of the river which separated them from their homeland and ordered to cross it, which in their eyes amounted almost to sacrilege: they must have shown signs of uneasiness which had to be dispelled. Hence the symbolic offering in which the mounts of some of Caesar's horsemen were called upon to play their part. Are we to take it that all his troops showed themselves to be satisfied and reassured? This is hard to believe. Caesar had no doubt had to use methods of individual persuasion, overcoming resistance and objection at the last moment, while taking care not to reveal too soon the true extent of his intentions.

No more decisions about "facts" are made. We are not told whether or not Caesar "indubitably" talked about the casting of dice, nor do we know that he hesitated. Having chosen only one "fact," the gesture of the horses, the biographer proceeds to move Caesar and his men across the river itself. Here he relies on the evidence of a poet, Lucan, whose story "is much nearer the truth than the spectacular scene imagined by the historians." There was no bridge—

> There could be no question of Caesar's waiting to construct a bridge. He remembered the method he had used in Gaul for crossing the Allier in almost similar circumstances. As before, the cavalry formed a barrack to check the current, and then, by an accessible ford, the infantry "easily made a passage through the already broken waters."

The quote is from Lucan himself, who has also given a set of circumstantial evidence to establish in the scene an immensely swollen Rubicon:

> The Rubicon rises in a small spring and its currents run feebly when the heat of summer beats down upon them, but the winter gives strength; rain and the Alps, meeting at the damp breath of Eurus, had swollen its waters.

Lucan is also the source of a speech that the biographer accepts, having thrown out, however, "the colloquy which Lucan introduces at the last moment between Caesar and the 'giant phantom of the Homeland in distress.'" The acceptable words were Caesar's:

> when, after crossing the river, he set foot on the opposite bank: 'Here I bid farewell to peace and outraged justice. It is thee, O Fortune, whom I follow. Away with treaties! Let us surrender to destiny! Let War be our judge!'

Then the narrative ends with a paragraph of only one sentence, one fact for which apologetic seems unnecessary: "The date was January 12, 49, at dawn." [6]

The construction of this narrative upon conflicting testimony involves the writer in a range of feelings of certainty. The degree of certainty he feels varies from the undefended date (all his sources must have agreed on this) to his suspended judgment on "The die is cast." Much of what he has accepted seems almost a matter of personal taste (like Caesar's speech on setting foot upon the opposite bank of the river), and some of what he has accepted comes

---

[6] Gerard Walter, *Caesar*, trans. Emma Craufurd (New York: Charles Scribner's Sons, 1953), II, pp. 19-21. Reprinted by permission of Charles Scribner's Sons and Cassell and Co., Ltd.

defended with fairly complicated inferences (like the swelling of the river and the ceremony of loosing the horses). Anyone who tries to construct the simple facts that go into historical narrative will discover that the knot of inferences is always at least as distorted as in the Caesar example.

A still more trivial example of how the historian's mind functions in the creation of little facts can be brought from my own experience. I have been working on this problem: how did twenty-eight volumes of Irish manuscripts get moved from the library of Sir John Sebright's London townhouse to Trinity College, Dublin, in the eighteenth century? I shall not attempt to justify my need for this information; it fills a place in a larger story. I have two facts ready-made: (1) they were reported to be at Sebright's in 1765; (2) they were in Trinity College in 1786. Sebright must have been persuaded by someone to present them as a gift to the College. They must have gone by sea. It is apparent that the process of inference begins immediately. Then my imagination starts to function. I see some faceless man in flowing cape and breeches, at the bow of a ship crossing the Irish Sea; I hazily visualize the ship; I picture a sea chest at his feet; I see gleaming silver buckles and white silk stockings against the dark chest; the chest is crammed with bound volumes, some parchment, some paper, some both; there are brown leather bindings with boards and ladder spines. This pictorializing comes partly from common knowledge about the eighteenth-century ways of doing things, partly from convictions about the behavior of inanimate objects in all times and places, and partly from modern reports about the appearance of the manuscripts themselves—for they are still in Trinity College. I also have some evidence out of which I can make a story; for instance a letter to Edmund Burke, whose correspondence I have been reading in Sheffield, England. The writer of the letter says, "Where are the two volumes of MS I brought from Leland to you 5 years ago? Sir John Sebright says he will not relinquish his collection until they are returned." "Leland" is Dr. Thomas Leland, whom I know to have received two volumes of Irish manuscripts from Edmund Burke in 1769—I have seen a letter of that year in which Leland thanks Burke for sending them. I shall not attempt to erect here the grandiose structure that is supposed to prove that the two volumes were Sebright's, that they had indeed been given back to Burke, that he had failed to return them to Sebright as late as 1781, that Sebright had indeed refused to give up the other twenty-six in his collection until he had got back the first two volumes, and so on. It is all done by imaginative leaping from probability to probability, grasping at swinging shreds of evidence that may be moved from one probability to another. I can never get on solid ground and walk around behind the manuscripts as they move through twenty years of the eighteenth century. But if I find enough peaks sticking up out of the clouds, I can create the illusion of solid ground. That is the best that can be done.[7]

It is not very helpful to have men like R. G. Collingwood and Benedetto Croce tell me that if I really worked properly, I could "rethink," "relive," or "reenact" the past with certainty. They tried to save "verifiability" in historical work by assuring us that since thought is peculiar to men and somehow is never lost in the universe as material things are, we can (and must) revive it. But I think they just try to frighten us into thinking we can really do that, by using depressing terminology. They talk of breathing "life" and "spirit" into "dead" documents and "empty" narratives. Croce pictured bad historians as morticians caring for embalmed bodies, never knowing how to revive them. He talked of contemptible (but indispensable) people like philologists, archaeologists, and archivists, busied with caskets and dried flowers, moving through "the silent white abodes of the dead"—that is, libraries, archives and museums.[8] Collingwood complained that our history was only "scissors-and-paste" unless we had "reenacted" past thought, as he did when he dealt with Lord Nelson at Trafalgar:

When I understand what Nelson meant by saying, "in honor I won them, in honor I will die with them," what I am doing is to think myself into the position of being all covered with decorations and exposed at short range to the musketeers in the enemy's tops, and being advised to make myself a less conspicuous target. I ask myself the question, shall I change

[7] The letters quoted and alluded to are in the Fitzwilliam Papers, Central Library, Sheffield, England. For their use I thank the Earl Fitzwilliam and the Trustees of the Wentworth Woodhouse Settled Estates.

[8] Benedetto Croce, "History and Chronicle," in Meyerhoff, *op. cit.,* pp. 52, 55-56.

my coat? and reply in those words. Understanding the words means thinking for myself what Nelson thought when he spoke them: that this is not a time to take off my ornaments of honor for the sake of saving my life.[9]

Actually if we forget the morbid imagery and the play-acting of "reenactment," we will find that what Collingwood and Croce describe as mere fact-getting, scissors-and-paste, chronicling, all that "dead" and "empty" historicizing, does fit quite well what historians in fact try to do. Collingwood and Croce seem unable to bear the idea that what they touch remains dead; but the past is irretrievably dead, and we can reconcile ourselves to this by putting it in kinder colors—for instance, we might say that we all move in a kind of perpetual autumn, where leaves die and fall continuously (and beautifully) into the accumulating past. We rearrange them in piles on the ground and imagine what the trees from which they hung were like, but we never try to make them green again except in imagination.

It seems to me that the two main problems about facts are fairly well settled. Facts are only sketchy constructions from some evidence and they are likely to be generalizations rather than true particulars. Therefore their "truth" is merely opinion or judgment, only as good as the thought processes that create them from evidence. Once the historian faces the fatal flaw in his work, that the past is gone and that perfect verification is therefore impossible, he should be able to return to his historicizing with confidence. There is no reason to fall into the mysticism of Croce and Collingwood; his imagination will serve him quite as well whether he believes it possible to communicate directly with the past or not. If he does not believe this, he will perhaps be better prepared to face the results of other historians' imaginations when their constructions turn out to be contrary to his.

II

Now let us leave the area of facts and move to some of the problems of "interpretation." This area is more puzzling and much

[9] R. G. Collingwood, *An Autobiography* (London: Oxford University Press, 1939), p. 112. Reprinted by permission.

less subject to settlement. The work of those who write about the problems of truth in historical interpretation attracts less agreement than what Becker and thinkers like him have said of facts.

An interesting and continuing discussion in this area is concerned with what is now being called "the logic of explanation" in history. The discussion has narrowed to a question of whether or not all historical explanation depends upon generalizations or laws. Most historians and critics have decided that there are no laws of events that determine the whole course of history, such as those of the great schematizers Toynbee and Spengler. More than that, the current dogma that history deals with the unique (while other disciplines are concerned with the general) has made it seem to many thinkers that historians have nothing to do with general laws. Yet critics point out that even the most innocent-sounding explanation may hang by a thousand threads from generalizations, many of them so trivial and commonly assumed that they have become invisible. Patrick Gardiner, for instance, suggested that what Collingwood imagined to be the rethinking of Nelson's thought at Trafalgar was nothing but an elaborate deduction from minor, commonsense laws about how men behave in battle, feel about their medals, and so on—rules about human beings which most of us assume and act upon without needing to make them explicit.[10] But are there "covering laws" for all inferences we make about the causes of past events? Some analysts are trying to find out by looking for other logical structures in historical work—structures that do not depend on such laws.[11] It is suggested, for instance, that no general rule is implicit when I say that Sir John Sebright waited to give his manuscripts to Trinity College until the two he had lent out were returned. I have the word of a contemporary that Sebright maintained he would not give them until the first two volumes were returned. I then infer that the two volumes were returned to him and that he then gave all twenty-eight to Trinity College. The inference depends upon my belief that I "understand" Sir John Sebright. I do not assume any rules about human nature, nor about all Sebright's ac-

---

[10] Patrick Gardiner, *The Nature of Historical Explanation* (London: Oxford University Press, 1952), especially pp. 115-17.

[11] The best example is William H. Dray, *Laws and Explanation in History* (London: Oxford University Press, 1957).

tions. I simply say he must have refused to make the gift "because" he was angry about the missing first two volumes, and "because" he intended to use the possibility of the gift as a weapon for getting the two volumes back. The causes that I cite are not based on rules; I do not reason "All men would be angry if two volumes of Irish manuscripts had been borrowed from them and not returned; Sebright was such a man . . ." etc. Rather I am making a kind of prediction, rather like a prediction I might make about a friend, saying, "I *know* him; I *understand* what he does; I know the unique causes of his behavior." I use my perception of the "nature" of this man, the hint that two volumes had not been returned, and from these I make my explanation, my interpretation.

I am not altogether sure that this argument proves the point. There may still be general rules lurking in my thought about Sir John Sebright. The whole question of explanation, historical and otherwise, needs a good deal of work. Either we always need general rules in our reasoning to conclusions or they are unnecessary in some kinds of thinking. It is certainly clear that a lot of historical writing is done without making any rules explicit, but whether some are really there—implicit—or (more important) some *ought* to be there, is a question we can expect to be debated further.

Even if the question of rules in explanation can be well enough analyzed in the future to reach answers as settled as those on facts have been, there will still be much more to worry about in the area of interpretation. Many analysts do not seem to realize that not all explanation indulged in by historians is *causal* explanation. With this in mind, I have been scrutinizing the histories I read, and have been surprised at the scant number of facts—the tiny amount of mere description—rattling around in the bottom of paragraphs and pages of elaborate causal explanation—why this happened, why it did not happen in some other fashion, what were its immediate causes, what were its deep underlying causes, what have been its effects, and so on. Even the most superficial-looking narrative, which seems at first to be sheer description, often turns out to be a series of causes that are linked implicitly by the words "And so . . . and so . . . and so," instead of "And then . . . and then . . . and then." But I think that many historians embark on voyages of interpretation that are not causal explanation at all.

In the first place, there are signs that historians are giving up all schemes that assign an over-all structure to the whole of the past: not the grand theories of Toynbee and Spengler, with their laws of repetition in human affairs; nor the supreme intuitions of God's plans displayed by Christian theologians; nor the transparently arbitrary schematics of the Marxists; but the structure implied by the current platitudinous metaphor, "The Web of History." Earlier generations imagined an endless concatenation of events through time, events linked together in causal chains. Even the modest interpreters, though sure that no Toynbee or theologian or Marxist could infer his system from the evidence, continued to envision the whole past as a structure that a God could see, if no mortal can. They imagined themselves, and the entire team of historians—the "profession," if you will—working to fill in a sketch of the parts of that structure, the way paleontologists work with their handfuls of bones to reconstruct some lost mammal. I rather think such assumptions are left-overs from that nineteenth-century historicizing mentioned earlier; the vision of a perfect history which would necessarily explain everything dies hard. But there are signs of its being given up. A reviewer, for instance, comments on the naïveté of so recent an historian as G. M. Trevelyan, who published yet another version of his *History of England,* mainly written in the late 1920's. The reviewer smiles at Trevelyan's simple arrangement of English history as a story of "progress"—a march of mankind up a steadily inclined plane. "The correct view of history, . . ." he says, "may well be as the meaningless scatter of stars in the heavens or the random flight of birds which we can do no more than describe." [12] If such were indeed the "correct view," or if historians began to write as if it were, we should expect to find them describing patterns of events, without trying to link them into a grand structure.

That historians are in fact beginning to work from such a point of view is clear from what is becoming standard treatment of "periods." The workaday historian who tries to show a class the "unity" or the "pattern" of a "baroque" or "medieval" period has probably left causal explanation behind, as he traces elements of baroque or medieval "style" from architecture to painting to music

[12] *Times Literary Supplement,* August 7, 1959, p. 460. Reprinted by permission.

and literature and even to government, philosophy and science. He is making a series of comparisons to give a kind of pattern to a period, but he does not try to trace the exact course of the "baroque" or the "medieval" from area to area; he does not try to explain how or why it so moved. The historian looking for such pattern simply sidesteps causal explanation, because he has begun to believe that there are other kinds of significance, unless of course he thinks of baroque or medieval style as a sort of all pervasive cause—a literal "spirit of the times."

Or, to take another example, a few historians seem to be presenting "views" of the past for their aesthetic value, detaching some events from their contexts, never considering whether or not they have a place in any over-all structure. For instance, Robert Brentano has written a book with the alarming title *York Metropolitan Jurisdiction and Papal Judges Delegate (1279-1296)*. It seems at first a conventional piece of work, as he explains the church government of the thirteenth century and tells the story of a series of intricate law suits from 1279 to 1296. But then it gradually dawns upon the reader that these things are subsidiary to what really interests the author: he is charmed with the snatches of "real life" (if this is not too hackneyed a phrase) which he imagines to glimpse through his pile of parchment, mostly compiled for thirteenth-century law courts, not for historians. He expresses it this way:

As one follows Wickwane [the main character of the book] about in his attempt to establish his authority in Durham, and then as one observes the growth of the excited disturbance that his attempt caused [this is the story, the explanatory narrative], one becomes involved in various ways in the daily life and thought of the thirteenth century. The people, whom one watches, move over bridges and across sands, sleep in white chambers, throw stones at horses, say Masses in chapels, and drink beer until they are sick.[13]

Brentano tries to give his readers a sense of how he has built these snatches of "life" from his strange materials (and all the vignettes

[13] Robert Brentano, *York Metropolitan Jurisdiction and Papal Judges Delegate (1279-1296)* ("University of California Publications in History," Vol. LVIII, Berkeley and Los Angeles: University of California Press, 1959), p. vi. Reprinted by permission.

mentioned are from his text), and so several of the aged materials are reproduced in the appendix. He wants to "involve" his readers in thirteenth-century life, but he also wants to "involve" them in the processes of discovery by which he is able to reveal his bits of thirteenth-century life. The effect is of a sort of mosaic, or perhaps a collage, where he has held his productions up for us to see; he calls our attention to the materials from which they are made, and their "pastness" is simply a part of the aesthetic effect. The "significance" he seeks most seriously is not explanatory, but is rather (I think) the aesthetic "significance" of a painting.

If historians should start to work out a wider range of significances like these and recognize that they do so, then they would perhaps begin to agree with Aron when he says, "History cannot give a final, universally valid account of societies, epochs, and extinct civilizations, for the very reason that they never had a unique and universally valid significance." [14] A world of significances may be seen in human existence, past or present, he says. If you go to the trouble (or through the excitement) of creating the remains of past events into facts, you might well prize them for their richness, rather than for their places in the great "concatenation." As the historicizing mania wears out in other areas of thought, it is beginning to wear out in historical work itself; and we may expect, I hope, some more history in a new key.

Suggested Readings

Barraclough, G., *History in a Changing World*. Oxford: Basil Blackwell Ltd., 1955.

Gardiner, Patrick, *Theories of History*. Glencoe, Ill.: The Free Press, 1959.

Geyl, P., *Debates with Historians*. New York: Meridian Books, 1958.

Popper, K. R., *The Poverty of Historicism*. London: Routledge & Kegan Paul Ltd., 1957.

Stern, Fritz, *The Varieties of History*. New York: Meridian Books, 1956.

[14] Raymond Aron, "Relativism in History," in Meyerhoff, *op. cit.*, p. 160. Reprinted by permission.

Literature and Reality

Walter A. Strauss

A problem as vast and baffling as that of literature and reality deserves to be treated with modesty and diffidence. Only a few salient points will be touched on in this essay, whose point of orientation will be a contemporary attitude toward the problem, rather than a general survey. The premise from which I shall proceed will be that in the past one hundred to one hundred fifty years the relationship between literature or beauty, on the one hand, and truth or reality, on the other hand, has been significantly altered.

A contemporary German poet and critic, Hans Egon Holthusen, opens his investigation of the problem of beauty and truth by asking a number of pertinent questions. Noting that the truth in poetry is something other than the truth pursued by science, philosophy, or theology, he declares that truth in poetry is a truth that "appears only *in* the Beautiful or *through* the Beautiful." Then he asks,

In what precisely is the particular "truth" of a poetic creation to be found? Is it found uniquely and exclusively in the plenitude of meanings of the artistic configuration, or is it found in a definite message that the poet wishes to convey to us? Has the poet really any message at all in mind except the one contained in the beautiful form of his creation? And again: can there even be a form that is not the form of something, the form given to a content, to a theme or to a substance? [1]

These problems are fundamental problems of aesthetics in our time; more so than ever before, since for us everything has become problematic. It is almost surprising that Mr. Holthusen should

[1] Hans Egon Holthusen, *Das Schoene und das Wahre* (Munich: R. Piper and Co., 1956), p. 5. Reprinted by permission.

raise the problem in terms of the traditional categories of beauty and truth. Evidently our age feels that the Keatsian equation (though it is here taken out of its proper context),

> "Beauty is truth, truth beauty,"—that is all
> Ye know on earth, and all ye need to know

is no longer satisfactory. We somehow feel that when we are witnessing the marriage of the True and the Beautiful (with Plato as justice of the peace), that it is really the Good—his bourgeois dignity outraged—that is lurking in the background, aiming a shotgun. Edgar Allan Poe and his French followers tried to keep the Platonic Trinity at bay with the definition that poetry is "the rhythmic creation of Beauty"; and Baudelaire, while admitting the seductions of Beauty, insisted that Beauty can be the instrument of diabolic forces:

> . . . ton regard, infernal et divin,
> Verse confusément le bienfait et le crime.
> (*Les Fleurs du Mal:* "Hymne à la Beauté")

It seems to me that after a century or so of challenge-and-response, neither the term Beauty nor the term Truth any longer holds the same significance that it had for Keats, and the Good has definitely bowed out of the picture altogether. This does not mean, however, that the Good has ceased to exist, but rather that its abode is now regarded as being outside the province of Beauty. The modern artist, as a general rule, is reluctant to talk about "Truth"; if he mentions the word at all, he means truth, or truths; and the word Beauty, although it seems to persevere, has been tinged with a Baudelairean *tristesse* that has definitely altered the profile of the goddess and revealed the moths in her drapery:

Je ne prétends pas que la Joie ne puisse pas s'associer avec la Beauté, mais je dis que la Joie en est un des ornements les plus vulgaires, tandis que la Mélancolie en est pour ainsi dire l'illustre compagne, à ce point que je ne conçois guère . . . un type de Beauté où il n'y ait du *Malheur*.[2]

[2] Charles Baudelaire, *Oeuvres* (Paris: Bibliothèque de la Pléiade, 1954), p. 1196. Reprinted by permission.

The problem of the interrelationship of the two categories—the True and the Beautiful—needs to be reexamined in our time. Since the late eighteenth and early nineteenth centuries we have acquired the habit of thinking—or rethinking—our problems in the sciences as well as the humanities in terms of *organic* relationships and *inner tensions;* thus our understanding of the arts has shown a similar inclination to focus on the "integrity" of the created work. Northrop Frye's observation, "a poem's meaning is literally its pattern or integrity as a verbal structure" [3] is not only characteristic of our attitude toward poetry, but to prose as well as music, painting, sculpture, and the dance. It has by now become a truism that form and content in a work of art are (or should be) aspects of an integral unity, but the question still hovers over us how such intuitions of unity can become significant as discourse about a work of art. Thus the question of beauty in a work of art also becomes a question of perspective, not of formulation; and "beauty" is here understood in Baudelaire's extended sense, which includes the melancholy and the grotesque.

But the question of "truth" and art continues to plague us. Certainly the "truth" of a work of art is not the same kind of truth that a scientist or a philosopher or theologian searches for. Heidegger has recently made an attempt to redefine art and truth in his essay on the "Origin of the Work of Art." [4] He defines the nature of art as follows: "das Sich-ins-Werk-Setzen der Wahrheit des Seienden"—the truth of that which is, setting itself to work (i.e., into the work of art). But not the truth of the individual thing, not imitation in its raw form. "The work of art is not concerned with the representation of the 'general nature of things,'" but with a revelation of the truth of Being within the things that are. To be sure, Heidegger's essay is an attempt to see the problem of art and truth in terms of Heidegger's own philosophy of Being, but regardless of this particularity and despite the difficulties inherent in the argument, the problem has been approached from an angle that suggests

[3] Northrop Frye, *Anatomy of Criticism* (Princeton: Princeton University Press, 1957), p. 78. Reprinted by permission.

[4] "Der Ursprung des Kunstwerkes," *Holzwege* (Frankfurt: Klostermann, 1950), pp. 7-68.

the possibility of a coherent redefinition, within a broader philosophical scope.

At the present time the word "reality" appears to be more viable than the time-honored word "truth." We have become increasingly suspicious of "truth"; it seems that the philosophers have found the term too useful in the past, and the scientists not useful enough. It strikes me that at this juncture of history the scientist is not so much after truth about phenomena as he is after methods of grasping the relationships among phenomena. The artist, who in his own way attempts to grasp the symbolic relationships within his experience, is not so vastly different from the scientist in this respect. The writer makes his experience refer to what he prefers to term "reality," since this word includes the subjective component of experience. Actually, the scientist *qua* scientist operates with his sign-equations and the artist *qua* artist with his symbol-equations. In the sense that both science and the arts belong to the general complex of human inquiry, neither scientist nor artist is ever completely detached from other human enterprise (thus the slogan "art for art's sake" is at the same time a tautology and an impossibility). Here Northrop Frye is helpful once again when he refers to literature as "a body of hypothetical creations which is not necessarily involved in the worlds of truth and fact, nor necessarily withdrawn from them, ranging from the most to the least explicit." [5] In the sense in which the artist involves himself and his creation in the world of reality, he may very well claim that he has some valid observations to make upon human experience and upon the world; and that the artist, after all—whether his name be Homer, Dante, Shakespeare or Yeats—has always had his special vision of reality. The only difference between Homer, Dante, Shakespeare, and Yeats is that the three earlier poets could count upon some *consensus gentium* among their readers, and the modern poet can count only upon limited agreement and understanding. In any case reality is the domain to be explored by the modern writer, not to be delimited: the modern poet's universe is open—toward the bottom and the top and even deep within: strange and vertiginous spaces surround and penetrate it. For this reason the modern writer's explora-

---

[5] Northrop Frye, *Anatomy of Criticism* (Princeton: Princeton University Press, 1957), pp. 92-93. Reprinted by permission.

tion, as measured against the survey of the world conducted by the "classical" poets, is tentative, bold, and ambiguous. The method employed is that of applying the language of symbols to the world that is to be grasped. Thus the symbol has been forced to carry a heavy burden by the modern writer.

"Symbol" is defined by Webster as "that which stands for or represents something else; a visible sign or representation of an idea or quality, or of another object, by reason of natural aptness, or association, or of convention; an emblem. . . ." But the modern writer goes beyond this definition in claiming that the symbol is in itself a kind of hieroglyph in the mysterious reality that he is trying to grasp. William York Tindall describes the symbol as follows:

Symbol, as we know it today, emerged during the romantic movement, which is best understood perhaps as an attempt to recover the upper half of the broken chain and, uniting it with the lower, to create something like the lost world of the Middle Ages and the Renaissance. The upper half of this restoration, however, required new meanings. Not only the place of spirit, it came to mean the imaginative, the subjective, the unconscious, or sensibility, separated by that famous dissociation from fact and reason, which continued to occupy the lower half of the chain.[6]

This is really the same thing that Erich Heller comments on so eloquently when he characterizes modern literature as the pursuit of the ontological mystery.[7]

A good example of how a relatively straightforward symbol may be used to produce complexity can be seen in Ibsen's *Wild Duck.* Here we have an object upon the stage that is both itself—a "real" wild duck—and a number of symbolic representations of the object. In keeping with the demands of characterization, Ibsen makes the wild duck symbolize something different for each of the characters. For Werle senior, Old Man Ekdal is like a wild duck because "There are people in this world who dive to the bottom the moment they're winged, and never come up again." Gregers melodramatically and grotesquely transforms the image of the wild duck tenaciously clinging to the tangle of weeds into an analogy with the Ekdal

[6] William York Tindall, *The Literary Symbol* (New York: Columbia University Press, 1955), p. 38. Reprinted by permission.
[7] Eric H. Heller, *The Disinherited Mind* (New York: Meridian Books, 1959), p. 17.

household, stuck in what he calls a "poisonous swamp" and identifies himself with the retrieving dog. He in turn persuades Hjalmar
to identify himself with the ill-fated duck in order to liberate himself by following the "claim of the ideal." Hedvig identifies with the
duck in still another way—the bird is for her the image of her own
loneliness and dereliction. Gina, the most sensible and unmystical
person in the Ekdal household, does not understand why there is so
much fuss about a household pet. And Dr. Relling, the specialist in
"saving lie" therapeutics, sees the wild duck as a toy for Old Ekdal
with which to perpetuate and romanticize a past that is more
bearable than the dreary present. But, hovering behind all these
functional presentations of the symbol of the bird, there is Ibsen's
own symbolic treatment—the use of the bird as a symbol of man's
loss of energy and nobility: the duck, once wild and proud and
free, is now the visible image of the modern city-dweller: fat, useless, domesticated—a bitter reminder of their greater and nobler
past for men who have become spiritless and disinherited.

Ibsen's handling of the symbol assumes meanings in the context
of this reality that he is communicating to us, and in this instance
the frame of reference is still definable in terms of discourse. When
we get to a representative twentieth-century writer, such as Kafka,
we can see that the ambiguities of the symbol not only multiply but
remain unresolved; we cannot assign clear meanings to the parable
"Before the Law" (Chapter IX of *The Trial*) the way we can in
Ibsen. The difference between *The Wild Duck* and *The Trial* is also
a difference in the use of irony. In Ibsen the irony resides primarily
in the tension between reality and appearance as it manifests itself
in the characters; in Kafka the irony is predominantly metaphysical
(with only a minimum of "psychological" components), arising out
of a tension between truth and reality. When Kafka lets Josef K. and
the priest make their own exegeses of the parable, one interpretation tends to cancel out all or most of another interpretation, with
the result that Josef K. is sadly forced to conclude that thus "lying
becomes a universal principle." But here too we understand that
Kafka's purpose is precisely to show that in a world stripped of
verifiable significance, everything becomes ambiguous and all talk
becomes double-talk. In this case the symbol has all the characteristics outlined above, except that there is no longer anything to

signify. In his parable about parables Kafka defines, with the utmost ambiguity, the discrepancy between truth and reality:

. . . All these parables [of the wise men] really set out to say merely that the incomprehensible is incomprehensible, and we know that already. But the cares we have to struggle with every day: that is a different matter.

Concerning this a man once said: Why such reluctance? If you only followed the parables you yourselves would become parables and with that rid of all your daily cares.

Another said: I bet that is also a parable.

The first said: You have won.

The second said: But unfortunately only in parable.

The first said: No, in reality: in parable you have lost.[8]

It would be hard to see paradoxical irony carried to further extremes; yet in a sense, this has been the temper of modern literature from Friedrich Schlegel to Samuel Beckett.

The foregoing examples of Ibsen and Kafka were intended as examples of two modes of treatment of reality as understood by the two authors and communicated to the reader primarily by means of symbolic presentation. The reality in each case, as Proust observed in his essay on aesthetics at the end of *A la Recherche du temps perdu,* is a vision that obsesses an author and gives a psychological unity to his work. The task of the artist as Proust understands it is to learn to read "le livre des signes inconnus" and to create a whole world out of the inwardness of sensibility and memory. Attractive as this position may be—and I might add that all literature and art since the Romantic period has been moving in this direction of inwardness, and the monuments of this secret architecture of the artists' souls are the glories of modern literature—it points up the loss of genuine relationship with the outside world. In a sense, as Mr. Heller observes shrewdly, music is the characteristic art of our time—the most unconcrete, the most inward of all the arts. From the late string quartets of Beethoven—a world that implies silence—to the late works of Anton von Webern—a world composed of silences; from the still life pictures of Chardin to those of Cézanne and the abstractions of Mondrian, the history of the

[8] Franz Kafka, from "On Parables" trans. by Willa and Edwin Muir. Reprinted by permission of Schocken Books Inc. from *Parables and Paradoxes.* Copyright 1961 by Schocken Books Inc.

modern creative imagination lies before us as a sequence of worlds made up of "silence, exile, and cunning." From Novalis to Baudelaire, from Mallarmé to Rilke, from Proust to Kafka, the vision has become one of increasing inwardness, precariously held together by a series of paradoxes—a literature of immanence.

In using this term I am coming close to the problem of literature and belief. Eliot, Heller, and Holthusen have debated it back and forth, and I should simply like to add that any so-called "suspension of belief or disbelief" seems to me to be a kind of self-inflicted handicap. All art requires total dedication in order to be fully experienced. The man who can suspend belief or disbelief is functioning only partially. The condition of all creative artists who matter is that they are concerned with themes that matter. What matters is man's relationship to himself, to others, to the world, and to God. If the particular vocabulary with which the artist treats these topics is not your own, you simply have to make the effort to learn it. What is required is not a suspension of disbelief but a reorientation of the vocabulary and syntax with which you are accustomed to interpret the world.

This leads to the question of criticism. The function of criticism is first to find out what is actually there, what pattern underlies it, and how this pattern relates to experience. What is actually there often necessitates the assistance of scholarship (so much maligned in our time); what pattern underlies it is close to the objectives of formal and structural criticism; and how it relates to experience involves intellectual history and reaffirms the bonds of art with the other disciplines—science, history, philosophy, and theology. The first two objectives are concerned with problems intrinsic to the study of literature, the third objective is extrinsic to it. Without the intrinsic criteria literature would merely be the handmaiden of some other discipline and thus lose its integrity; without the extrinsic reference literature would merely be a series of personal visions in a void and thus lose its integration. It is in this spirit that the words of Salvatore Quasimodo from his *Discorso sulla poesia* carry a particular resonance:

The position of the poet cannot be passive in society; he "modifies" the world. . . . His forceful images, those that he creates, beat on the heart of man more than does philosophy or history. Poetry is transformed into ethic, precisely because of its beauty: its responsibility is in direct proportion to its perfection. To write verses means to undergo judgment: and implicit in the aesthetic judgment are the social reactions to which a poem gives rise. We know the reservations one must make on these statements. Yet a poet is a poet when he does not renounce his presence in a given land, at a precise time, politically defined. And poetry is the freedom and truth of that time and not the abstract modulations of sentiment.[9]

Our age is admittedly an age of criticism—too much criticism, as Randall Jarrell regretfully remarks. But criticism—which is a manifestation of the human impulse to analyze and comment—is fundamentally no more than the phenomenon of human inquisitiveness and the desire to engage in discourse about something that is of human significance. The problem for criticism in our time is to reassert its bonds with the scholarly tradition and with the total scope of human inquiry. In the process it will also have to define the limits where historical and technical inquiry shades off into the analysis of the cultural situation. As Ezra Pound put it,

General formulas of art criticism serve at best to suggest a train of thought, or a manner of examining the individual works of a period. Such formulas are not figures circumscribing the works of art, but points from which to compute their dimensions.[10]

In this way, literature and the arts reaffirm their claim to serve as the instruments of preserving, interpreting, and transforming human experience, by means of the passionate commitment of the feelings and the intelligence to the representation of the total human situation, contemplated in its manifold aspects and rendered with all the honesty and skill that the creative artist can muster.

Suggested Readings

Auerbach, Erich, *Mimesis.* New York: Doubleday and Company, Anchor Books A107, 1957.

[9] Salvatore Quasimodo, *Writings,* ed. and trans. by Allen Mandelbaum (New York: Farrar, Straus, and Cudahy, 1960), p. 14. Reprinted by permission.

[10] Ezra Pound, *The Spirit of Romance* (New York: New Directions, n.d.), p. 166. Reprinted by permission of New Directions, Publishers.

Blackmur, R. P., *Language as Gesture*. New York: Harcourt, Brace & World, Inc., 1952.

Block, Haskell M., and Salinger, Herman, eds., *The Creative Vision: Modern European Writers on Their Art*. New York: Evergreen Books E224, 1960.

Cassirer, Ernst, *An Essay on Man*. New York: Anchor Books A3, 1953. *The Myth of the State*. New York: Anchor Books A52, 1955.

Frye, Northrop, *Anatomy of Criticism*. Princeton: Princeton University Press, 1957.

Heller, Erich, *The Disinherited Mind*. New York: Meridian Books M66, 1959.

Hulme, T. E., *Speculations*. New York: Harvest Books HB41, 1961.

Langer, Susanne K., *Philosophy in a New Key*. New York: New American Library MD101, 1951.

Richards, I. A., *Practical Criticism*. New York: Harvest Books HB16, n.d.

Tindall, William York, *The Literary Symbol*. New York: Columbia University Press, 1955.

Truth in the Study
of Religion

William A. Beardslee

Truth is a worn-out word, as the earlier papers in this series remind us. The sober scholar of today does not claim that he is dealing with ultimates. Yet religion deals with ultimates. What of the scholar of religion, the student of man's immediate awareness of the ultimate?

In the first place, the student of religion is not exempt from the situation in which, today, we see that all students find themselves. The limitations of human perception and thought in the face of reality, the unclear and unexamined nature of most of our language, the relativity of our grasp of life and value to our position in history and in society—these are the lot of the student of religion as of any other scholar. A century ago, an Anglican theologian could write to John Henry Newman, disconcerted by the latter's move toward Rome, "I am ready to grieve that I ever directed my thoughts to theology, if it is indeed so uncertain as your doubts seem to indicate," [1] but the hundred-odd years since Archdeacon Wilberforce wrote his anguished letter to Newman have been marked by a steady retrenchment, on the part of Roman Catholic, Protestant, and Jewish theology alike, of the claim that theology can provide the kind of objective certainty which Wilberforce took for granted. Indeed, Newman himself is a profoundly prophetic figure in his recognition of the oncoming wave of relativism and his foresight into its dissolving effect upon religion.

But the tension between scholarship and faith is not simply a re-

---

[1] From a letter of January 29, 1842, by Archdeacon Robert I. Wilberforce, quoted by John Henry Newman, *Apologia pro Vita Sua* (London: Longmans, Green, and Co., 1887), p. 163.

sult of the contemporary intellectual situation. The attitude of scholarship itself, not only in our time, but in any time, and carried out with any intellectual apparatus, is a procedure which by its nature creates a certain distance from the reality to which religious awareness opens itself. Not for nothing have religious men recurrently been suspicious of scholars, and though we may attribute the anti-intellectualism of much contemporary faith to its unwillingness to adjust to certain widespread social and intellectual changes, this resistance has profound religious roots as well. For the religious life claims a validity which can be known only immediately, and when one makes it the object of scholarship, he in a measure inevitably destroys it. John Bunyan wrote, "Of all the temptations that ever I met with in my life, to question the being of God and Truth of His Gospel is the worst and the worst to be borne." [2] Here speaks the authentic religious life; but the life of scholarship, even when scholarship does not assume a stance of neutrality which is actually indifferent, in Bunyan's words, to "the being of God and Truth of His Gospel," nonetheless by its making the religious an object of study, inevitably removes it from the realm of its own proper immediacy. And when scholarship is carried out in a humanistic setting, it inexorably proceeds to that point which the genuinely religious man identifies as the worst temptation to be borne, namely, the doubting of the being of God and of His Truth. Not only in our time of relativities, but in any time, the scholarly study of religion sets men at a distance from religion and thereby threatens the vital life of religion, as well as, in its very process of analysis and construction, making the real understanding of religion more difficult as its forms become clearer.

The recognition of these difficulties has led increasingly to the demand that we stand within faith to understand it. Religion, indeed, is a pejorative term nowadays, because it suggests that we are dealing with a human phenomenon, and in particular because religious men are dissatisfied with that understanding of faith in terms of religious experience which marked so much of the pietistic religion of the nineteenth century. The path to understanding through faith is a valid and significant one, and we shall return to it. But if

---

[2] John Bunyan, *Grace Abounding to the Chief of Sinners*, Conclusion, No. 1.

we undertake to *understand* religion, we must join interpretation from within the circle of faith to interpretation within the context of human experience and awareness. Understanding requires both participation and distance. Communication about faith is in good measure limited to a particular group of believers, when understanding springs only from the circle of faith. This limitation of understanding is not absolute, for, as will be noted below, the languages of faith can also be understood at least partially by those who do not share their presuppositions. But quite apart from this difficulty, it is part of the nature of understanding that it requires us both to unite ourselves with that which we seek to comprehend, and also to hold it away from us to view it. Hence in the context of this series it is appropriate to begin with the study of religion as a phenomenon, as something to be observed.

But this way of understanding is of vital importance for religion's sake as well, for this reason: our world is characterized by a striking erosion of immediate awareness of the divine. It is a profoundly secular world, not only in its intellectuality but in its life, and while the crisis of our time is making men sensitive to their need of faith, the littleness and angularity of so much of the faith and theology which we see today testify that religious men, too, do not know the depth and scope of religion. The study of religion thus stands in a sort of alternating relation to religion itself—while study creates distance, thus weakening the immediacy of faith, it may also create awareness, an awareness, indeed, which may constrain the student to a different sort of engagement with the religious reality.

We turn, then, to the study of religion, and propose that we may approach the understanding of religion through discourse in three kinds of "language." By speaking of distinct "languages" we do not imply that thought is identical with language. Nor do we mean, as will be apparent, that any one of these realms of discourse is exempt from criticism in terms of another, although this mutual criticism is subject to the limitation that the matters under discussion cannot be grasped with equal comprehensiveness in the different languages. Furthermore, we do not mean to suggest that the "languages" we propose are the only coherent systems of discourse which may be used to discuss religion. Nonetheless, such a way of putting it will suggest approaches to religious reality which have validity apart from this particular terminology. Thus we may discuss religious matters in public language, in contemplative language, or in convictional language.

There is not much to say about the use of public language in communicating about religion. Here truth means verifiability in ways that can be identified publicly. In this case, the human element is the element that contributes to error, not to understanding. "Public" does not mean generally accessible, but testable by public methods. The truths of this language are not ultimate, for reasons that need little elaboration.[3] Aspects of religious reality are accessible to study in public terminology, but only in a fragmentary way. In the tradition of religious scholarship, linguistic studies are a good example of those techniques which come close to this sort of definition. Studies of the meaning of a word, for instance, are statistical and probabilistic in nature, even though in lexicography we have not been able to quantify and mathematicize our methods to the degree achieved in many other fields. There is a public probabilistic truth about the meaning of a word on which there can be a general consensus, yet the limitation of this definition of lexical study at once becomes apparent when one notes that the alternative meanings are not ultimately reducible to the public realm—they inevitably carry a symbolic freight which makes lexical study, for all its objectivity and public character, an art rather than a science. At best, public language can make affirmations about the function of certain elements of life that are related to the religious. It cannot disclose the nature of the religious, to say nothing of the nature of God—and furthermore, since the functions which it studies are always multiple functions in which the religious is related to other things, the study of religion by methods which are approximately reducible to public language has on the whole tended to lose sight of the religious dimension; or to put it differently, the religious eludes this sort of study. Nonetheless, those aspects of religious behavior and thought which are accessible to this sort of study need to be subjected to it, and it has repeatedly supplied a check on unwarranted conclusions reached by other methods.

Secondly, we turn to what we have called contemplative lan-

---

[3] See the essay by J. H. Goldstein earlier in this volume.

guage. By this term is intended simply coherent discourse about what the religious reality *appears* to be, leaving aside the question of its truth—or what van der Leeuw designates as phenomenology of religion.[4] We call it contemplative language to indicate that in this approach religion is contemplated; it is observed as a human phenomenon. This sort of study can and must supplement the insights of the man of faith. Here human understanding of patterns or structures makes possible a grasp of the phenomena of religion as living wholes, and makes possible as well a classification of them into types. Such study is uncommitted—not by believing, but by imaginative participation, is understanding achieved—yet it is of course true, as van der Leeuw notes, that the phenomena cannot be grasped by one who is unconcerned, and a person who had no awareness of the religious could not really engage in this discourse.[5] Yet a student's awareness would not have to be committed awareness for him to be able to know what he was talking about. He might, for instance, be a former believer. Indeed, by contemplation one can perceive and imaginatively enter into forms of the religious life which are vastly different from one's own. It is precisely this possibility which constitutes the immense importance of the study and sympathetic observations of religion as a phenomenon. I must say, parenthetically, that I have been somewhat baffled by the spirited rejection of Collingwood and Croce at an earlier point in this series, for they are, of course, with respect to human existence in general, advocating a kind of human understanding of which the imaginative participation in the religious is a special type. This method does not naïvely identify our experience with that of another. Rather, as van der Leeuw finely observes, such study is conscious of the fact that not only the ancient Egyptian or the Pacific Islander and not only every neighbor, but even my own past self is separated from my understanding by an immense gulf.[6] What I create in understanding is not the thing itself, but a distant and artificial structure of understanding which makes me aware both of the fact that understanding is possible only because of a common humanity,

---

[4] Gerhardus van der Leeuw, *Religion in Essence and Manifestation,* trans. J. E. Turner (London: George Allen and Unwin, 1938), pp. 671-93.

[5] *Ibid.,* p. 675.

[6] *Ibid.,* p. 677.

and also of the fact that the other's experience into which I place myself is something foreign, distant, and different.

For the student of religion the ultimate difficulty with human insight and imaginative comprehension does not lie in the limitations of "empathy," real as these are. It is true that such understanding is fragmentary; it can only in part, and usually in small part, be checked by recourse to studies which can be carried out in the public language—linguistic or sociological studies, for instance. But no one who has seriously studied the reality known as the religious can doubt that the method has validity. It can produce a typology of religion, which enables us to see and order the phenomena of religion and by ordering them to enter into them imaginatively more deeply and adequately. But—and here is the greatest limitation of this method from the point of view of religious studies—by its nature the method is relativistic or pluralistic. It can expose to us, and put in some order, the manifold religious life of man, and it can enable us to appreciate it better. It can show us what is real in the sense of what men have found real in their confrontation of the ultimate. It is perhaps a symptom of our position that van der Leeuw so defines phenomenology of religion as to exclude God.[7] But even if God be included as the object of disciplined inquiry, still we do not move beyond a pluralistic view. Norms can, of course, be elicited from such studies—one might, for instance, conclude that certain religious types were more effective than others for certain purposes. Certain types might be more beneficial to society, for instance. But no ultimate norms appear to be accessible to this sort of study. The most it can do is to present and to order the ways in which men respond to the religious.

Now this is no small achievement, and it is one which can have a peculiar significance in our own time, as we have noted above. Many of those who can most powerfully communicate their grasp of what life in our time is, cannot identify the religious dimension in it. They may nonetheless be concerned with the religious and be in fact one of our most important sources for understanding the religious. The very absence of the explicitly religious, in the works of sensitive and powerful imagination which spring from our situation, is a testimony to the dying out of the religious from the

[7] *Ibid.*, p. 688.

forms and structures which in our society were formerly its principal bearers; or at least—for this is also part of the picture—the inaccessibility of the genuinely religious that maintains itself, often in irrelevance to the needs of men, in the structures of religious form. But our great artists are also, for the most part, men of religious concern. The denial of religion may itself be a religious act, and the affirmation that God is inaccessible may be a cry to Him. Thus the vision of the religious quest as it presents itself, usually in baffling inconclusiveness, in the art and writing of our time, is a prime source of understanding of the religious. But this avenue of understanding, powerful because drawn from a contemporary vision, needs to be placed in the context of a wide human understanding of religion, not merely to avoid losing ourselves in the moment, but to enable us to see the fragmentary movements of religious life in their setting. We may cite one specific example: phenomenological study of mysticism will do much to help us see the significance of themes that recur increasingly in art and writing today, and will make it possible for us to ask questions about the implications of the vision of reality which we find in the art of our day, which need to be asked from the point of the understanding of religion, even though they may not be central to the study of the works of art themselves.

Furthermore, as already noted, contemplation of the phenomenon of religious encounter can in real degree deepen the student's awareness, and thus enable him to grasp a dimension which easily eludes the modern reader. The example below comes from Koinonia Farm in Americus, Georgia, which is an "intentional community," —a group which has tried to reshape the whole pattern of its life according to a truly Christian model. It is against this background of earnest rejection of common cultural values that the following story, which describes the arrival of a new family at the Farm; is to be read.

[A new couple], with their five daughters, came to Koinonia through a rather unusual experience. They were visiting relatives in Kentucky at the time, and [he] says that while he was praying he received a very strong leading to go to some people in south Georgia who were trying to live as did the early Church described in Acts 2 and 4. He had never heard of either Koinonia or Americus, nor were these names given to him at the time. The leading was so strong and persistent, however, that he packed his family into the car and set out to look for these people. As he came into Georgia, he began to inquire here and there if anybody knew of such a group, the name of which he did not know, nor the place where they were located. Little by little he was led nearer, until he finally arrived at our driveway, where he found things exactly as he had previously described them to his wife and children. Not yet sure that this was where God wanted him to settle down, he pushed on into Florida. Once again the leading brought him back to Koinonia, with the feeling this time that this was home.[8]

To contemplate, to observe with an imagination disciplined and trained by observing other phenomena of religion, will reveal here not merely the obvious questions about social nonconformity and the psychology of religious experience—questions that we most easily hear, and which we may of course legitimately explore—but also a level of response to what is perceived as ultimate and holy, here seen in a form of an ethical command. Who, once he has seen this response of faith, can fail to perceive that here is a form of human confrontation of the ultimate which needs to be understood in order to understand man, and who indeed can observe it, suspending commitment in order to grasp it the more fully, without also some sense of longing—a sense of longing which indicates the not yet wholly personal nature of the language of contemplation and of the study which is its counterpart?

We turn now to the language of conviction. "Convictional language" (Willem Zuurdeeg's term) not only expresses the fact that this language is grounded in a conviction or commitment but also conveys the fact that the person who speaks convictional language understands himself to be "convicted," to be grasped by that to which he gives himself.[9] Such language is basically religious language, but convictions, often unexamined or unconscious, also deeply permeate our ordinary speech. Though we often suppose that ordinary conversation is nontechnical public language and deals with public matters, this is only partly the case. Much of the diffi-

[8] *Koinonia Newsletter*, No. 22 (November 1, 1959), p. 3. Reprinted by permission.
[9] For the term "convictional language," and for insights reflected in the following discussion I am indebted to Willem F. Zuurdeeg, *An Analytical Philosophy of Religion* (New York: Abingdon Press, 1958). But I do not concur in Dr. Zuurdeeg's rejection of metaphysics or in his limitation of philosophy to the role of analysis.

culty we have in understanding each other in everyday matters arises from the unexpressed convictional elements in our discourse, which often are in conflict not only between persons but between different aspects of one person's convictions. For this point of view we see that the ways of understanding and communicating here termed "public language" and "contemplative language" are in fact artificial languages created for certain special purposes.

Commitments run through the whole life of man, insofar as it is personal and responsible. To the degree that university life consists of study, it moves away from convictional language toward contemplative language or public language. Indeed its major task must be carried out in these less personal languages, even though the final basis for the various intellectual tasks lies in a commitment of some sort. The reserve with which, even in the intellectual life, we approach the commitment-bases of our various tasks is partly the result of a natural reticence to disclose what is most dear to us. But here again our own intellectual situation intensifies a general tendency. The reader of this series can hardly fail to be struck by the way in which a group of scholars, each presenting the way in which his subject grasps reality or truth, largely refrain from claiming for their areas an ethical dimension. This scholarly reserve stands in strong contrast to the earlier overmoralizing of many realms of intellect. We may sympathize with the resistance to what we now see to be an oversimple and overrigid moralism. But whether the resulting current trend—which appears so clearly in the earlier essays of this series—to find broader meaning in the field by means of an aesthetic rather than by an ethic, will ultimately prove more adequate than the earlier fashion, remains to be seen.

At any rate, though the religious, the commitment to the ultimate, has in our tradition more usually been seen as a term beyond the ethical, the fact that the religious may equally well be viewed as a term beyond the aesthetic reminds us that the newer trend is not necessarily less relevant to the quest for religious meaning than the earlier, ethical way of finding meaning, even though the kind of religious meaning that appears will be different.

About convictional language as such the first thing to be said is this: that it is possible to communicate with it. This fact can be disputed, by saying that men can communicate only if they agree about their commitments. Certainly, convictional speech is most effective when it proceeds within a community, and by far the largest part of the discussion of truth and meaning which takes place is carried out on the basis of at least a measure of common commitment. Furthermore, our commitments effectively exclude us from some kinds of understanding. By venturing to be conventional members of society we to some degree exclude the possibility of fully understanding what it is to be a "beatnik." By the act of faith in Christ we exclude the possibility of entering to the full into certain other sorts of religious understanding. And of course these prior commitments are not simply chosen; they are subject to many limitations which also limit our consequent understandings. Not everyone can *choose* to be a gnostic; many of us are too earthy.

Nonetheless, a measure of real communication, and a consequent measure of real common consent about truth, are actually achieved across convictional lines in convictional language. For one thing, there are elements in common between alternative forms of conviction, between Christianity and Islam for example, or even more clearly between Christianity and Judaism. Beyond those common elements lies the fact of the common humanity of all men whatever their commitments. Real, though limited, communication is possible, resulting either in the discovery of a common element in alternative commitments—a "general truth"—or in a change in commitment because one is seen to be inadequate; although often, of course, the outcome can be no other than the clarification of basic differences.

There are many modes or degrees of convictional language. We can distinguish the modes of *proclamation* and *theology*. The immediate language of faith directs itself to men as the former—the language of appeal, the confrontation with the ultimate and holy in such fashion that the listener is constrained to decide for this truth.[10] Possibly the distinction between proclamation and theology is not valid for all religious languages: some forms of faith, for instance, may lack the aspect of appeal or proclamation. But the

---

[10] Religious language includes the form of divine speech as well as man's speech about God. For a discussion of an aspect of divine speech, see Martin J. Buss, "The Language of the Divine 'I,'" *Journal of Bible and Religion*, XXIX (1961), pp. 102-107.

distinction is an important one for our purpose, as a reminder that within the circle of faith or the community of faith, theology is a secondary language, engaged in, in a certain sense, only when the faith becomes a question. Theology stands in a relation of alternation to the more immediate language of proclamation or "preaching." By clarifying the meanings of faith and by relating faith to the whole of life, theology makes the proclamation of faith more effective. Thus theological truth is truth which arises from reflection on the meaning of the commitment to the ultimate.

The most important problems of theological truth in our time relate to the withdrawal of God from the world and from the established structures through which God was traditionally known. In the intellectual sphere, the inability of the mind to reach ultimate reality is a commonplace of our day, well summarized by Tillich when he says:

Knowledge stands in a dilemma; controlling knowledge is safe but not ultimately significant, while receiving knowledge can be ultimately significant, but it cannot give certainty.[11]

The involvement of man in the relativity of social time is keenly felt today, so that even his theology can at best be the grasp of the ultimate as it appears and meets our situation, and not a pure grasp of the ultimate. Hence theology must always be done over. There is no ultimate theology, even though theology is perennially concerned with the ultimate. Most perplexing of all is the inability of the clearer modes of thought to deal with responsibility. The public language can discuss sequences, but it can say little that is significant about responsibility. We sense that responsibility should be responsibility *to* someone, yet we find it difficult to identify that with which we are to enter into a responsible relation. We find ourselves in a world in which God is not available. God is not an existent, like other existents, yet increasingly existents are all that is available to us.

---

[11] Paul Tillich, *Systematic Theology*, Vol. I (Chicago: University of Chicago Press, 1951), p. 105. Copyright 1951 by the University of Chicago Press. Reprinted by permission. "Controlling knowledge" is Tillich's term for knowledge achieved by holding oneself at a distance from the object known; "receiving knowledge" is his term for the knowledge which unites itself with what is known.

Theological thinking may ignore this situation, as traditionalist theology, both conservative and liberal, does. Indeed there is a measure of justification in its doing so, for we need to remember that for all the talk about the human situation in which the modern man finds himself, there is no one human situation, and there are those for whom traditional theologies are relevant and authentic. The failing of such theologies is that they are not—if I may use a traditional religious word—sufficiently missionary. They fail to become engaged with the human situation as it is discovered by those who cannot find meaning in the traditional formulations. In this respect the attempts at theological reformulation, which are widely regarded from the traditional point of view as concessions— giving in to the nonreligious conception of the world (and there is a measure of truth in this valuation)—are more properly to be seen as attempts to allow the religious proclamation to be heard in the present situation. The sacrifice of some of the intellectual securities of traditional Christianity is to be understood on the lines of the saying, "He that loseth his life shall find it." There must be, at certain times in the history of religion, a withdrawal and pro- tection of the faith from the world; and apart from the specific intellectual issues which are involved, one of the live questions of contemporary religious life is the debate, often not articulated in these terms, between the position that would protect the faith from the assaults of the world, and the posture that would give itself into the chaotic and meaningless situation of our time.

Theological thinking which tries responsibly to confront the situ- ation of man in the postscientific world is an exceedingly lively and varied enterprise. Theologians differing as widely as Barth, Bultmann, Tillich, and Buber have all affirmed that the absence of God from the world which man can control is not to be regarded as a simple sign of the decay of the world of faith. Rather the recognition of God's absence from this area opens the way to a new discovery of the meaning of faith, since the God who is known by man's controlling knowledge (Tillich), or God known as an "it" (Buber) becomes an idol. Thus such theologies are faced with the problem of speaking of a God who does not exist as other things exist.

We may illustrate by referring briefly to the Christian theologian

Paul Tillich and the Jewish theologian Martin Buber. They have much in common, and neither represents a pure type—each is heavily influenced by that character of thought which I am about to say is predominantly the mark of the other. Yet we may take them as representing two great types of modern theology.

The mystical type springs from an immediate awareness of the absolute. Tillich's religion of the absolute is modified by its strongly historical-personal element. But it reveals, as one of its central elements, a religious awareness of being encountered by the unconditioned, that which is abyss as well as ground. This mystical theme affords a principal way of reaffirming the reality of faith, for Tillich holds that "controlling knowledge" cannot touch the reality of such immediate awareness of the absolute.

The ultimate direction of such a theology is a gnostic transcendence of selfhood. Tillich's own theology keeps the gnostic-mystical element, with its absolute God, in check by relating it to the concrete, personal encounter with the Christ. The tension between these elements, the mystical and the personal, is a reminder that analysis by types, for all its usefulness, cannot always be an ultimate criterion in the language of commitment. That is, a given way of interpreting a faith may be irreducible to a simple type, and may resist the efforts to reduce it to theoretical simplicity. On the other hand, one of the primary tasks of theological reflection is to be sure that the different aspects of the given faith are actually compatible, and to determine where its true center lies. Many of the students of Tillich are baffled to know whether his theology centers in an absolute or in a personal God.

Such a theology as Tillich's is significant in our time for its strong emphasis on the religious as the dimension beyond existence, and thus ultimately unchallenged by that technical or controlling reason which has removed God from the visible world. It has significance as well for its restatement of religious themes in the spectrum of concerns beside the ethical, in a world which has grown tired of moralism and easily dismisses the religious as nothing more than the ethical. Tillich is also significant, whether one agrees with his particular way of doing it or not, as a theological thinker who even in a time of intellectual disorientation still grapples with the task of making intelligible the relation of faith to the whole round of knowledge. This theological task is easily displaced today by the urgent need to stress the uniqueness of faith. But the synthetic task which Tillich undertakes is one to which theology will have to return.

While many of the same things can be said of Martin Buber, of special significance here is the renunciation of the mystical for the intensification of responsive, responsible encounter—what I call the personal, though this term is also used in other senses. On the side of man, Buber's way of letting himself be apprehended by the divine emphasizes as strongly as possible the concrete, active, choosing, unique man; on the side of God, in spite of the decisiveness, as strong in Buber as in Tillich, that God is not an object, his theology affirms that God is not the absolute but is characterized by the seriousness with which he encounters man. God is Thou. He is involved in a dialogue as a man is involved, and hence both the understanding of man and that of God preclude the ultimate goal of the doing away of the barriers of concreteness. The holy is met always in encounter.

To the threatening prison of relative, man-structured reality Buber responds not with an immediate grasp of the absolute, but with a personal, responsive relation between man and the divine Thou. There is today a reaction against personal-historical faith, which sees the religious as "beyond" responsibility but has often degenerated into mere moralism. Much contemporary religious thought and life is turning either to an appreciation of mystical faith—a faith which does not center on personal existence—or else to a (closely related) awareness of the holy as something "beyond" aesthetic experience. Buber instead intends to reopen an understanding, in our own situation, of that form of awareness of God which has always been central to the Judeo-Christian tradition. The narrowness of an ethical definition of faith is overcome by a rediscovery of the power, freedom, and love of the divine Thou who stands, even when forgotten or when He withdraws, as the real basis of responsibility. The nature of communication in convictional language is well illustrated by the fact that themes analogous to Buber's, and indeed his own direct influence, are a marked feature of much contemporary Christian thought, which also characterizes the coming of God to man in terms of an

"I-Thou" encounter. Jewish and Christian thought each sees in the other a structure similar to its own, yet each must testify that in its own concrete historical-personal foundation of faith (Jewish or Christian) it finds the decisive base for the continuing life of faith.

In both Tillich and Buber we have impressive statements of the way in which theological affirmations can be true. They are true to the situation of men in our time, accepting and entering into its chaos and dislocation and refusing to identify God with any objectively verifiable reality; they are true in the sense that they represent the ultimate concerns of serious men who, even in the vacuum of our time, allow themselves to be encountered by the religious and affirm that this encounter is real, and that God is real. But of course for the observer this truth is pluralistic. Ultimately the mystical and the personal cannot be fused, and one is exposed to both and confronted with the necessity of choosing between them, as also with the framework of the personal-historical one must open himself to the power of a given focus of divine encounter—the Covenant or the Christ. Yet this varied truth is not mere subjectivity or relativeness, for each position can recognize elements of truth in the other and enter into conversation with it. To this discussion not only the analysis of language, but also the broader criticism of philosophical theology, will make its contribution. Finally, these theologians remind us of the constant nature of theological discourse, which exists in order to make more effective and penetrating the religious language of proclamation— "Choose ye this day whom ye will serve."

Suggested Readings

Herberg, Will, ed., *Four Existentialist Theologians.* New York: Doubleday and Company, Inc., Anchor Books, A141, 1958.

Buber, Martin, *Eclipse of God.* New York: Harper Torchbooks, 1952.

Otto, Rudolph, *The Idea of the Holy.* New York: Galaxy Books, 1958.

Bultmann, Rudolph, *Existence and Faith,* trans. Schubert F. Ogden. New York: Living Age Books, 1960.

Myth and
Symbol

Myth in Myth

Robert L. Scranton

Sisyphos: toiling up his hill; struggling, laboring, to lift his burden to the height, only to have it slip from his grasp when success is almost his, and plunge to the foot of the hill where once again he must begin anew his eternal task.

No one knows now what this story of Sisyphos meant to those who first evolved it around the hill of Akrocorinth fifty centuries or more ago, but through the millenia since then it has survived, carrying now one meaning, now another. Once perhaps, it was understood as an account of an aspect of the seasonal struggle of life and death; once, as a lesson in divine justice; today it re-emerges as a statement of man's life in an existential world. What is the truth? Or, what is the relation of myth to truth, if there *is* truth? Could we say, in still a new interpretation, that the story of Sisyphos is the truth about truth—that when our whole concentration of effort brings us to the presence of truth, the goal dissolves only to reappear once more as a new beginning?

The following essays are concerned with the meaning of myth or symbol in certain aspects. Speaking with reference to several kinds of problems, and with several kinds of approaches, they all reflect the realization that communication—perhaps even understanding—cannot be really immediate or direct, but must be through devices that are in some sense symbolic, and that myth is an important device of this kind. The essays do not agree entirely in their conception of myth and symbol and the relation of these to each other or to rational or objective formulations of truth, but it is not the purpose of this essay to analyze the problems they raise. Our task is rather to focus attention on myth as myth, independent of the particular problems of understanding it in contemporary study of religion, philosophy, literature, or social science. We shall try to recall the nature and role of myth in mythology as a starting point for what is to follow, and, perhaps, as a basis for some synthesis.

The question, of course, concerns the strictly "mythic" part of "mythology," not the legendary material or the "Märchen" or fairytale. The distinction is indeed difficult to make: memories of things past, and fabrications of the imagination to divert a long evening, can at least be formally defined though not always so easily recognized, but the accounts of the forces at work in nature and man that we might choose to designate "myth" are not even easy to define verbally, let alone to recognize in their elusive form, behind their anthropomorphism, and amid the shifting influences playing among the various kinds of folklore.

At least it is possible to maintain that myths were narratives, however brief; they were accounts of some kind of happening. And if we wish to link myth intimately with "symbol" we must distinguish between other kinds of symbols and a "mythic" symbol, perhaps by saying that the myth is a narrative, the symbol is a verbal or visual figure drawn from myth. Both of them possess some quality in common that distinguishes them from other narratives and other figures, and this quality resides in symbols by virtue of their origin in myths. A flag that marks a point in a road where people are to turn or stop, or the word "mother" as a designation of a female of a species in a particular physiological-sociological set, may indeed be designated "symbols," but this symbolism is of a different order from that of the flag inspiring men to heroic action, or the word "mother" comforting by evoking the warmth, security, fruitfulness, possessiveness, protectiveness that are a value in life in general. It is the second kind of meaning, the extra meaning by which the visual figure or the word provides power as well as information, that our kind of symbol, as distinguished from other figures, has in common with myth as distinguished from other narrative. To be sure it is not actually the *word* "mother" itself which is symbolic in this sense, but the woman herself as evoked by the word. And woman may be not mother, she may be rather lover, in which case she is again a powerful symbol. And, of course, she may be both, and the tension of the essential impossibility of this, the emotional incompatibility, with the inescapable fact that she is indeed both, gives the woman as a symbol even greater force. But what makes the woman symbolic we may not actually know simply by looking at her; we know it ultimately because of her role in some sequence of events—her myth.

The tension resulting from multiple and even contradictory meanings of "woman" is a quality of myth, but this much may of course be felt in personal experience, in natural drives heightened by psychological complications—the stuff of which "psychological" novels are composed. In less introspective use, however, this particular symbol may be fully mythic, and even more powerful, by the fact that the tension we actually feel is felt also to be cosmic in scope: the sense that the "human" forces which drive us within are in fact the same as those which raise the tides and create the bloom of spring only to overwhelm it with the storms of winter. The concepts of "mind" and "Eros" as applied to cosmic order by the pre-Socratics were not simply poetic; they imply an attitude that the basic forces controlling the physical universe were of an order having some quality in common with those of human life. These early philosophers were not so naïve, of course, as to imagine the attraction among elements of the cosmos as a "falling in love" in a romantic or biological form. Rather they assumed that the emotional and physical manifestations of human love were an aspect of the same compelling attraction as pervaded the rest of nature, though they must have conceived of cosmic forces as having a kind of consciousness understandable in human terms. The cult myths, too, assumed that the processes of nature in general are in fact the processes of human nature: thus the myth of Oedipus and Jocasta, in addition to being an account of an intricate psychological conflict, is also a fusion of two cultic recitals of the cycle of life, one conceived as male, one as female, identifying human fate with cosmic process.

There is, of course, a tremendous unsolved question as to how, and why, this identification is possible. Has man projected his image on the universe, or has his image of the universe been stamped on his own understanding of himself, or was there, originally, any actual difference in his perception of himself and the universe? There is no room here to discuss these problems, nor is there a definite answer.

It is probable in any case that "genuine" myth originated in close relation to cult and ritual, though now we know it usually as folklore or literature, even of considerable sophistication. In the *Metamorphoses,* or the *Golden Ass,* of the second century after Christ, Apuleius tells the story of a man, Lucius, who is trapped by his licentious way of living into being transformed into an ass. After a lengthy period of degradation, exposed to all kinds of bestialities directly and indirectly—physical torment, sexual wantonness (narrated, to be sure, as a ribald picaresque)—he eventually achieves his goal of being transformed again into a man, through the intervention of the goddess Isis. This tale is a kind of fable, constituting an analogy to the real experience of the man himself whose conversion, through various ceremonies of initiation, from a life of evil into the purer, almost divine life of service to Isis, is also narrated. A more general meaning is imparted to the work by the story of Cupid and Psyche, introduced into the narrative of Lucius' adventures as a tale told by an old woman to a captive maiden in the power of some bandits who at one point possess Lucius himself, in his form as an ass. This story of Cupid and Psyche is narrated as a "Märchen," a folktale, a fairy-story, that is familiar to us otherwise as "Beauty and the Beast" but in Latin is a patent allegory since the names of the characters—Cupid and Psyche—are directly designated Love and Soul. So there is the story: Soul is one of three sisters, beautiful in body and spirit above all others so that she is beloved and admired by all, even to the point of being worshipped for her goodness as an incarnation of the goddess Venus. Venus, here, is an established proper name for the traditional goddess of Love and Beauty, but in the narrative to come the goddess evidently stands for love in the aspect of physical passion. Because, then, of the jealousy of Passion, Soul is maneuvered into being given as a sacrifice, but is wafted away by the winds to a magic palace where she mysteriously becomes the bride of Love. Her sisters find her, corrupt her mind with suspicion, so that she violates her pledge of blind fidelity and seeks to know who her husband is: in this loss of faith she loses him and is driven into a world of horror and affliction to find him again. Ultimately, after vile abuse from Passion and after penetrating even into the depths of death, she is found and saved by Love, with whom she lives happily thereafter. With the broad hint of this allegory, and the reverent apostrophes to Isis and the descriptions of the vision of Isis, we can feel no doubt of the really exalted message of this tale of the regeneration of the human spirit through the grace of divine love, while the direct story of Lucius' conversion and the bawdy exaggeration of the adventures of the Ass point out the same message in the language of fable and human experience.

The message is given a certain elevation by the obvious mythological and religious elements such as the prayers to Isis, the vision of the goddess and her message to Lucius, and other explicit religious expressions; and various allusions to the Olympian gods provide such elevation as the reader, with his particular background, may find in pagan religion. But there is also a nonexplicit mythic element which is only implicit in certain episodes, though sometimes a more or less casual allusion will alert the attention. Such, for example, is the quest of Soul to the land of the dead, and her being overcome by charmed sleep, before her resurrection and restoration to Love. More obscure is the significance of the episode just before the transformation, or conversion, of Lucius the Ass to Lucius the Man. First there is the obscene sensuality of his being brought to have, in his form as an ass, intercourse with the depraved rich woman of Corinth; then the repulsive crimes of the murderess; and then the plan to bring these two horrors together in the public punishment of the murderess by causing Lucius the ass to have intercourse with her publicly. But just before this public exhibition, in the theatre, is a colorful pageant of the "Choice of Paris" among the contending beauties of Olympus, displaying their charms in a more elegant though not essentially more elevated vision of physical love. But meanwhile Lucius has escaped to the seaside where his prayers are answered in an ecstatic vision of Isis, Nature, the Moon, the Universal Mother, Demeter, Aphrodite—the fructifying, vitalizing power of the cosmos—who now comes into Lucius the Ass to make him once again Lucius the Man. In this sequence of events the reader himself experiences the pattern of cosmic numinous process—the terrible, awful violence worked by the overwhelming power of nature, fertility, sex, love, as part of its process of re-creation and true life. In the harrowing experience of raw bestiality and corruption the real essence of humanity is purified and released.

In the simpler, starker, more concentrated literature of the fifth century before Christ the force of the myth is greater and more direct than in this artificially complicated work of later classicism, though perhaps still not easily perceptible in itself. It brings to the story of Oedipus and Orestes and the others, though presented as human experience, the power of the cosmic forces that they were in the primeval stages of their myths. And this is a peculiar quality of folk myth: to give another dimension to a concept—and not simply some other, but that which makes it one with the ranges of the universe beyond man; to show the concept in several aspects simultaneously, one of them human, another cosmic.

Although in our tradition myth has usually involved concepts of a god or gods, or all-pervasive numinous or animistic powers, it has proven a validity even in materialistic and mechanistic systems. In the world of the "absurd," even if the absurdities should be without animus and purely inert, they constitute the inseparable burden of man in the new myth of Sisyphos, by which a locus and rationale for man in the universe are given in categories of human experience. In the world of Marxism, though God and humanity are eliminated from the cosmos and society and even man himself, stubbornly myth persists, in giving dynamic direction in a world where the mechanics of nature and society operate in a "dialectic," a "proletariat" "dictates," and the ideal man is the proletarian hero who fulfils himself in the traditional mythic *pathos,* as society itself is saved, in the catastrophe of revolution and war.

In the Sisyphean task of establishing truth, or whether there is truth, many paths up the hill have been attempted. In the modern world in particular there has been a tendency toward exclusive confidence in one, the self-conscious "objectivity" which resists any bond between thinker and reality and regards suspiciously the imputation of anything "human" in anything "nonhuman." But such an attitude obviously is a limitation of the vision—it is to put on blinders which would make it impossible to see the truth if the truth should be of the peculiar complex nature which the mythic consciousness alone, because of its own resources and adjustment, could comprehend in rational form. If Sisyphos really wishes to succeed, he must be open to the possibilities of myth, as well as to other possibilities, that may lead him with his burden secure to the height.

The Religious Meaning
of Myth and Symbol

Thomas J. J. Altizer

I

Ever since the birth of the modern scientific and rational consciousness, a series of romantic reactions to the rational quest to
modern man has exalted the strange subterranean world of myth
and symbol. In our own time, the symbol has been baptized by the
rational consciousness itself and seized upon as the source and center
of human thought and feeling. Thus Ernst Cassirer has defined man
as a "symbol-making animal"; and has maintained that it is the
principle of symbolism which gives access to the specifically human
world, to the world of human culture.[1] The world of the symbol is
quite simply the world of human language, expression, and communication. Accordingly, it is through the symbol that the world
becomes open to human experience and understanding. So likewise
the symbol is the language of religion. Although religion expresses
itself through symbols, the religious symbol is not to be identified
with the symbol as such. For the religious symbol opens man to
a transcendent reality manifest in human experience. Only through
the religious symbol is this reality revealed to man; for, apart from
the religious symbol, man would remain enclosed within his own
immanence. Speaking of the religious symbol, Paul Tillich has said:
"This is the great function of symbols, to point beyond themselves in the power of that to which they point, to open up levels

Some of the material in this essay has been adapted from Thomas J. J.
Altizer, *Oriental Mysticism and Biblical Eschatology,* Philadelphia: The Westminster Press, 1961. Reprinted by permission.
[1] Ernst Cassirer, *An Essay on Man* (New Haven: Yale University Press, 1944),
pp. 23-26.

of reality which otherwise are closed, and to open up levels of the human mind of which we otherwise are not aware." [2]

A wealth of scholarly literature has already been devoted to the world of the symbol, and the student of religion has not been idle in this field. For the most part, and in accordance with their romantic roots, the religious studies of myth and symbol from Creuzer to Cassirer have focused upon the symbolic world of primitive or archaic man. Now this is a significant fact; for, as will be seen, there is a deep and significant difference between the role and meaning of symbol in the primitive and in the so-called higher religions. Regardless of how we conceive primitive man, it is obvious that primitive (or preliterate) peoples have a much more integral relationship with nature and the cosmos than do the highly self-conscious peoples of civilized societies. This truth has important consequences, as witness the work of Mircea Eliade, the most distinguished contemporary student of the religious meaning of myth and symbol. Eliade believes that, for the primitive, symbols are always religious because they point to something real or to a structure of the world: "For on the archaic levels of culture, the *real*—that is, the powerful, the meaningful, the living—is equivalent to the *sacred*." [3] It is just this identity of the real and the sacred that marks for Eliade the distinguishing feature of what he terms the archaic ontology, the basic presuppositions of the world of primitive man.[4] The religious symbol (and, in primitive culture, all symbols are religious) is both capable of revealing a modality of the real or a structure of the world that is not evident on the level of immediate experience, and is also capable of expressing simultaneously a number of meanings whose continuity is not evident on the plane of immediate experience. This means that ". . . the religious symbol allows man to discover a certain unity of the

---

[2] Paul Tillich, "Theology and Symbolism," in *Religious Symbolism*, ed. F. Ernest Johnson (New York: Institute for Religious and Social Studies, 1955), p. 109. Reprinted by permission.

[3] Mircea Eliade and Joseph M. Kitagawa, eds., *The History of Religions: Essays in Methodology* (Chicago: University of Chicago Press, 1959), pp. 98-99. Copyright 1959 by the University of Chicago. Reprinted by permission.

[4] Cf. Mircea Eliade, *The Myth of the Eternal Return*, trans. Willard Trask (New York: Pantheon Books, 1954).

World and, at the same time, to disclose to himself his proper destiny as an integrating part of the World." [5]

Again, Eliade notes that a symbol always aims at a reality or a situation which engages human existence. It is this human—what Eliade calls "existential"—dimension that distinguishes symbols from concepts.

Symbols still keep their contact with the profound sources of life; they express, one might say, the "spiritual as lived" *(le spirituel vécu)*. This is why symbols have, as it were, a "numinous aura"; they reveal that the modalities of the spirit are at the same time manifestations of life, and, consequently, they directly engage human existence. The religious symbol not only unveils a structure of reality or a dimension of existence; by the same stroke it brings a *meaning* into human existence. This is why even symbols aiming at the ultimate reality conjointly constitute existential revelations for the man who deciphers their message.[6]

All of this, be it noted, assumes an essential continuity between the religious symbol and the structure of the world: it assumes an ultimate identity between *reality* and the *sacred*. Furthermore, it is the religious symbol which integrates human existence into the structure of the cosmos: "The religious symbol translates a human situation into cosmological terms and vice versa; more precisely, it reveals the continuity between the structures of human existence and cosmic structures." [7] Consequently, the religious symbol makes possible the "harmonization" of man, the cosmos, and the sacred.

Although Eliade draws a radical distinction between the reality which is revealed in the religious symbol and the reality which is manifest in the world of profane experience, he believes that the religious symbol opens man to the real as such—to Being itself. Here, Eliade is in continuity with the classical Christian tradition which maintains that the religious Reality embraces or is manifest in all genuine reality whatsoever. Yet an important problem arises

[5] Eliade and Kitagawa (eds.), *The History of Religions*, p. 100. Copyright 1959 by the University of Chicago. Reprinted by permission.

[6] *Ibid.*, pp. 102-103. Copyright 1959 by the University of Chicago. Reprinted by permission.

[7] *Ibid.*, p. 103. Copyright 1959 by the University of Chicago. Reprinted by permission.

at this point. For modern man experiences both an alienation of himself from the cosmos, and an alienation of the *sacred* from *reality*. We can know neither a human existence integrated with the cosmos nor a sacred Reality in harmony with the reality of the world. This is true in our experience of the world as well as in our experiences of the sacred (for we inherit both Pascal's shudder in the presence of the cosmos and Nietzsche's proclamation of the death of God); likewise is it true in our understanding of the nature of the world and the nature of the sacred.

Therefore it is the purpose of this paper to challenge Eliade's correlation of man, the cosmos, and the sacred, in his understanding of the religious meaning of myth and symbol. For Eliade's identification of the religious symbol with the archaic symbol fails to account both for the meaning and role of symbol in the higher religions and for the meaning of the religious symbol in our historical situation. Our method will be to examine the meaning of the religious symbol as it opens itself to us at this juncture of history. In other words, we shall attempt to demonstrate that the meaning which is manifest in the religious symbol in our contemporary situation—as expressed in contemporary thought, sensibility, and religious scholarship—is in radical discontinuity with the symbolic meaning which is the product of man's life in the world, of his life in being.

II

The religious symbol appears through the language of myth; myth—or, more properly, myth-ritual—brings order, meaning, and structure to the world of the religious symbol. However, we must beware of identifying mythical language and rational language; nor must we assume that a mythical language will perform the same function or establish the same kind of meaning as a rational language. Moreover, mythical language cannot employ concepts; it must use images and symbols which resist all genuine rational meaning. Historically, *logos* arose through the collapse of *mythos,* and the man who lives under the spell of *logos*—that is, the men of the higher civilizations—can never fully enter the mystery of *mythos*. As the romantics of all periods have insisted, there is a mystery in myth which eludes the rational categories of scientific and historical analysis, as well, one might add, as the grasp of romantic philosophers and theologians. Indeed, it should be emphasized that the very word "myth" indicates a loss of the meaning —or reality—to which myth points. For a conscious awareness of the mythical as a distinct language arises only when man has established a gulf between himself and the sacred. The mythical appears as the "mythical" only when the reality to which it refers can no longer immediately be grasped.

In a certain sense, it is true that myth belongs to the world of archaic man. Certainly the sense of an integral relation between myth and reality, which is often taken as an essential sign of the purest form of myth, is a phenomenon to be observed only in the world of precivilized man. Furthermore, genuine myth invariably engages what one can only describe as an archaic sensibility: even if we postulate that such a sensibility lies buried in the unconscious psyche of rational and civilized man. This means that the reality to which myth refers can never be sensed as "real" by the modern consciousness. Hence the constant movements either to abandon myth or to restore it in yet another synthesis. Myth can in no authentic sense embody what the modern consciousness recognizes as truth: thus writers from Goethe to Tillich, who have insisted that the symbol must embody the reality for which it stands, have been diagnosing the inability of the modern mind to live in the world of the religious symbol. Consequently modern man is doomed to live in an a-mythical world. Although modern writers such as Joyce and Kafka have succeeded in constructing mythical visions, these visions embody either the absence of the sacred or the presence of a negative or demonic transcendence.[8] They are reflections of the religious void which lies at the center of a profane existence.

Human existence as we know it (Heidegger's *Dasein*, Sartre's *pour soi* and so on) is a mode of existence alienated from the sacred; our human reality—our consciousness—is a reality which we can sense only as wholly profane. Modern man, Faustian man, has chosen the goal of autonomous freedom: and this freedom can be reached only by means of a dissolution or negation of the sacred

[8] Cf. Walter A. Strauss, "Franz Kafka: Between the Paradise and the Labyrinth," *The Centennial Review*, V (1961), 206-22.

and the transcendent. Modern man becomes himself by a process of desacralization: as Nietzsche saw, he must become the murderer of God. Eliade himself has referred to this modern situation as a second Fall:

> From one point of view it could almost be said that in the case of those moderns who proclaim that they are nonreligious, religion and mythology are "eclipsed" in the darkness of their unconscious—which means too that in such men the possibility of reintegrating a religious vision of life lies at a great depth. Or, from the Christian point of view, it could also be said that nonreligion is equivalent to a new "fall" of man—in other words, that nonreligious man has lost the capacity to live religion consciously, and hence to understand and assume it; but that, in his deepest being, he still retains a memory of it, as, after the first "fall," his ancestor, the primordial man, retained intelligence enough to enable him to rediscover the traces of God that are visible in the world. After the first "fall," the religious sense descended to the level of the "divided consciousness"; now, after the second, it has fallen even further, into the depths of the unconscious; it has been "forgotten." [9]

Nor can we regard this eclipse of the sacred as an accidental phenomenon. The very Faustian quest of modern man (his basic goal of achieving absolute autonomy in every sphere of life; as Max Weber observed, the rationalization of Western culture and society has been equivalent to a process of desacralization) has demanded the eclipse—the "death"—of God. The only reality which modern man can know, as *reality,* is wholly profane: modern knowledge is Faustian knowledge; it arises out of the dissolution of the sacred. As is well known, a wholly new knowledge of myth and religion was evolved in the modern West. For the first time, knowledge "about" religion came into existence. But this new understanding of myth and religion is also a Faustian product of the Second Fall: religion (the very word "religion" testifies to the presence of a profane conciousness) became a human and historical phenomenon. Therefore even the myth and religion which we "know" is a product of desacralization; we have known religion only as a human and historical phenomenon, and not as the presence of the sacred.

Nevertheless, we have no choice but to live with our knowledge

[9] Mircea Eliade, *The Sacred and the Profane,* trans. Willard Trask (New York: Harcourt, Brace & World, Inc., 1959), p. 213. Reprinted by permission.

of religion. We cannot escape it, since it is embedded in our very destiny as modern men; and we may yet find that this knowledge too can bring liberation. For our knowledge has taught us that "religion" is in some deep sense wholly other than every other human phenomenon (as witness the vitually universal acceptance of Rudolph Otto's idea of the "numinous"). Thus twentieth-century studies of myth and religion have fully established that myth is not basically a literary or conceptual category. Myth is a primary mode of the religious response which in its origin cannot be separated from ritual. Van der Leeuw speaks for the majority of historians of religions in describing myth as a verbal celebration of a sacred event.[10] Myth, like ritual, is a mode of encounter with the sacred which makes possible the continuous re-presentation, or reevocation of a primal sacred event. Bronislaw Malinowski justly speaks of primitive myth as "a narrative resurrection of a primeval reality." [11] Myth is action as well as word; indeed, myth is the actualization of the primordial beginning (sacred time) or of the axiological center (sacred space) of existence. Furthermore, myth affects the whole man; and the explication of its psychological effects must deal with unconscious as well as conscious processes, as the work of Freud and Jung has demonstrated.

However, the word and action of myth can open man to communion with the sacred only by turning him away from the actuality and concreteness of his historical existence. The sacred can be actualized only by means of a dissolution or sublimation of profane existence. Nor is it accidental that the sacred can only be defined as the polar opposite of the profane. Myth can only actualize the primordial time of the beginning, or the axiological center of the world, through a dissolution of the categories and experiences of concrete time and space. When we study the effect of myth in a living religious community, we can see that myth succeeds in actualizing a primeval reality by continuously detracting its adherents from the concrete actuality of their daily lives. By its very nature myth dissolves the profane world of reality and opens its

---

[10] G. van der Leeuw, *Religion in Essence and Manifestation*, trans. J. E. Turner (London: George Allen and Unwin, 1938), p. 413.

[11] Bronislaw Malinowski, *Magic, Science and Religion* (Garden City, N.Y.: Doubleday and Company, 1954), p. 101.

participants to the transcendent world of the sacred Reality. The most distinguished modern studies of myth (Cassirer, van der Leeuw, Eliade) have demonstrated that myth negates the profane world of concrete time and space. "Mythical thinking," according to Cassirer,

> . . . comes to rest in the immediate experience; the sensible present is so great that everything else dwindles before it. For a person whose apprehension is under the spell of this mythico-religious attitude, it is as though the whole world were simply annihilated; the immediate content, whatever it be, that commands his religious interest so completely fills his consciousness that nothing else can exist beside and apart from it. The ego in spending all its energy on this single object, lives in it, loses itself in it. . . . This focusing of all forces on a single point is the prerequisite for all mythical thinking and mythical formulation.[12]

Here, the immediate experience should be understood as a response to the sacred Reality—re-presented by myth—which is so compelling in its power as to shatter, at least momentarily, all normal conscious experience. That is why myth can never fully be captured by means of a literary document; for it can never be dissociated from its effect on the believer, from ritual. In this perspective, myth and ritual are parallel expressions of one reality. They are simply the forms of the manifestation in human experience of the sacred Reality. Ritual effects what the myth represents so that myth-ritual is the reliving of all that is known as the numinous, the sacred, and the transcendent. Yet this reliving of the holy is only possible through a continual dying to the profane.

Modern studies of the religious effects of the Christian liturgy have demonstrated that the liturgical action of the Christian Eucharist makes the worshipper actually present at the Last Supper, the Crucifixion, and the Resurrection.[13] These primeval events of the Christian faith are made actual in the ritual actions of the liturgy. The Passion Story is the verbal celebration of this action, and it seems likely that it originally arose out of Christian worship (cf. Bultmann's treatment of the narrative of the Last Supper as a

---

[12] Ernst Cassirer, *Language and Myth*, trans. Susanne Langer (New York: Harper and Brothers, 1946), pp. 32-33. Reprinted by permission.

[13] Cf. Dom Gregory Dix, *The Shape of the Liturgy* (Westminster: Dacre Press, 1949), pp. 238-67.

cult legend[14]). Accordingly, the sacred events of Christianity—as of Judaism, too, for that matter—were recorded more deeply by means of myth and ritual than they were through the agencies of conscious memories or historical records. It has been well said that the Gospels are Passion Stories with extensive introductions. The Christian participates in the reality of Jesus through the mythical symbol of Christ and through the ritual action of Christian worship. Not concrete historical memories, but the mythical form of the Christ event and the living reality of Christian worship made possible the preservation and renewal of the Christian faith. This fact doomed to failure the nineteenth-century quest for the "historical" Jesus. In a profound sense there is no "historical" Jesus for the Christian, but only a "mythical" Jesus, because for the Christian believer Jesus is wholly a sacred Reality and in no sense a profane being. Today we can see that it was only when the original eschatological-mythical form of Christianity collapsed that a Logos and Incarnational theology arose which made possible the integral relation of Jesus to the world.[15] Insofar as Jesus is identified with the mythical symbol of Christ—which is the substance of the Christian faith—he can be reached only by means of a reversal or dissolution of the profane reality of the world. To have a consciousness of Jesus as an "historical" being is to live apart from faith. Indeed, the historical consciousness—as the scientific consciousness—arose only after and in conjunction with the secularization (or desacralization) of Western culture. Thus, to grasp Jesus as an historical or an objective phenomenon is to live in unbelief. Such a consciousness of Jesus could never arise except through the collapse of myth, which is but the symbolic form of faith.

III

No effort to present the meaning of religious myth should be regarded as complete without some effort to construct a typology

---

[14] Rudolf Bultmann, *Die Geschichte der synoptischen Tradition* (Goettingen: Vandenhoeck and Ruprecht, 1931), p. 307 f. I am indebted to Dr. William A. Beardslee for this reference.

[15] Cf. Martin Werner, *The Formation of Christian Dogma*, trans. S. G. F. Brandon (London: Adam and Charles Black, 1957).

of mythology. Even the best modern studies of myth suffer because they for the most part limit themselves to the analysis of primitive or archaic mythologies. This is true of Eliade, for example, whose conclusions are based upon the mythical world of what he terms the archaic ontology. Here, it is legitimate to speak of the cosmological dimension of myth and of the function of mythology in integrating man, the cosmos, and the sacred. But it must be remembered that the higher religions also express themselves by means of a mythical language: there are no proper grounds for limiting mythology to the religion of archaic man. Therefore the student of religious myth must attempt to comprehend in his analysis both the mythology of archaic man and the developed or refined mythologies of the higher religions. I would like to suggest that there are three basic types of religious mythology, arising out of (1) archaic religion, (2) mystical religion, and (3) prophetic-eschatological religion.

Let us follow Eliade in defining archaic religion as all that religion which lies outside of—both historically and geographically—the higher civilizations of history. For the present purpose, let us simply define higher civilizations as those that have evolved or assimilated rational thinking. One notes immediately that the mythology of archaic religion embraces the whole realm of natural phenomena. Although there are significant differences between the mythologies produced by preagricultural and agricultural societies (the former revolving about a Sky God and the latter about an Earth Mother), both are cosmic in orientation. We find myths of the sky, the sun, the heavenly bodies, the moon, oceans, lakes, rivers, stones, mountains, earth, and so forth.[16] Wherever man has an experience of the sacred he symbolizes it by means of myth, and thus makes possible its continual re-presentation. Clearly, the mythical symbolization of nature in archaic religion reflects archaic man's sense of harmony and communion with the cosmos. Nor should it be forgotten that the only higher religions which succeeded in maintaining this sense of harmony—Chinese religions and Far Eastern forms of Buddhism—never detached themselves from their archaic roots. Nevertheless, critical modern studies of archaic myth have demonstrated that myth does not comprehend nature *qua* nature

[16] Cf. Mircea Eliade, *Patterns in Comparative Religion*, trans. Rosemary Sheed (New York: Sheed and Ward, 1958).

(nature is never simply nature to archaic man, nor does he have an understanding of natural law or an abstract idea of nature) but nature as the area of sacred or numinous power. The mountain is not symbolized because it is a "mountain," but because it has provided the occasion for an experience of the sacred. In the same way, the religious function of archaic myth revolves about the re-actualization of either the sacred time of the beginning, or of the axiological center of the world. Archaic myth transforms the concrete time and space of profane existence into the archetypal time and space of the sacred beginning and the sacred center.[17] Here, the mythical symbolization of the mountain provides an entry into the archetypal center of existence. Yet this center is a transcendent Center: therefore it can only be entered by means of a turning away from—or a temporary "forgetting of"—the concrete world.

The mythical world of archaic man can by necessity be known by modern man only through mystical and romantic categories; for the archaic world is not open to "empirical" experience, insofar as "empirical" experience can be reached only through rational thinking: and to think in rational categories is to be closed to the archaic world. Thus, the presence of rational thinking dissolves man's openness to myth. But at this point a major distinction must be made. For myth is not confined to the world of archaic man: it is also found—although here playing a new role—in the higher religions themselves. First, note should be taken of the strange fact that the higher cultures of history burst into time almost simultaneously. Thus, in the midst of widely divergent geographical and cultural areas, and at a roughly identical period of time (eight to fourth centuries B.C.), can be seen the dawn of philosophy and of a higher aesthetic consciousness in Greece, the prophetic reformations of Palestine and Persia, and the birth of philosophy and a series of religious revolutions in India and China. These movements, which apparently occurred independently of one another, induced Karl Jaspers to call this period the Axial Period of history, insofar as he believes that it effected a transition from a Mythical Age to the modern period of the universality of history.[18]

---

[17] Cf. Eliade, *The Myth of the Eternal Return.*

[18] Karl Jaspers, *The Origin and Goal of History,* trans. Michael Bullock (London: Routledge and Kegan Paul Ltd., 1953).

In this period the fundamental categories were created which still lie at the basis of contemporary thinking: the epistemological consciousness, religious transcendence, the individual ethical imperative, the autonomy of selfhood, and so on. For the first time man became conscious of a gulf lying between himself and reality. Indeed, one might well be tempted to say that it was at this time that humanity as we know it evolved. Commonly this period is interpreted as entailing a struggle of *logos* against *mythos*. However, if *logos* and *mythos* are seen as antithetical categories, the victory of the new mode of understanding banishes *mythos* to the archaic world of primitive man, and therefore the higher forms of religion are seen as nonmythical. But it is manifestly true that myth is present in the higher religions.

Furthermore, the assumption that the higher religions embody some sort of primordial victory of *logos* over *mythos* obliterates the tension between the rational and the religious consciousness, and assumes that religious faith and understanding are founded upon an affirmation and understanding of the world. Yet one actually finds that all of the higher religions are world-negating, world-dissolving, world-reversing, or world-transforming; and all of them are in tension with the rational consciousness (and with the practical-historical consciousness as well) insofar as consciousness pursues a knowledge of and power in the world. The higher religions do not engage so much in a negation of myth, as in an elevation and transformation of the archaic mythical forms. Eliade terms this process an "interiorization" of the primordial mythical tradition: the religious goals of the archaic religion now become open to individual instead of communal experience, the mythical-ritual acts of the religious community are transformed into modes of experience and faith of the individual believer. Accordingly, this means that a genuine continuity exists between the so-called lower and higher religious forms. As Eliade insists: ". . . I should like simply to declare that almost all the religious attitudes man has, he has had from the most primitive times." [19]

Nevertheless, the higher religions are grounded in a revolutionary

[19] Mircea Eliade, *Patterns in Comparative Religion*, trans. Rosemary Sheed. Copyright New York: Sheed and Ward, 1958, p. 463. Reprinted by permission.

transformation of the archaic tradition, for they make possible a new openness to the sacred Reality, a new and immediate participation in the sacred which was not open to archaic man. Paradoxically this new participation arises out of a radical gulf that is now seen to lie between man and the sacred, a gulf which cannot be crossed by the archaic forms of religion. In the prophetic tradition, deity becomes the Wholly Other: a chasm is now seen to lie between the creature and the Creator; while in the mystical traditions (with the exception of China), the sacred Reality is banished from the world. Once the archaic religious forms become irrelevant to the religious quest, man can no longer meet the sacred simply by participating in a holy community: the very gulf between man and the sacred demands a radical individual and interior act of "turning" to the sacred. For the first time, "faith" comes into existence in the prophetic tradition, and parallel to it, individual acts of meditation are born in mysticism. But these new and higher forms of religion, if only because of their radical nature, make possible not only a more individual, but also a deeper participation in the sacred Reality. Inevitably, in this situation, myth assumes a new role and meaning.

Whereas both Chinese mysticism and Far Eastern Buddhism (including both Zen and Tantric Buddhism) pose special problems of their own due to their failure to break with the archaic religion, in the various forms of Indian mysticism we can see a clear example of the role of myth in the higher religions. *Brahman, Atman, Purusha,* and *Nirvana* are basic symbolic categories which have wholly detached themselves from their mythical roots. All of them express mystical revolutions against the archaic Indian religious tradition. In each case the symbol postulates a religious goal which cannot be reached by the traditional forms of myth and ritual, nor by rational or conceptual thought. All of them rest upon a dissolution of consciousness—for ultimately the mystic contemplates only the Nothing—which obliterates all experience of the world and the self. Obviously mystical religion revolves about an individual experience, which has passed beyond the ancient forms of myth and ritual. But if we look more closely we can see that the Yoga exercises, the foundation of Indian mysticism, reproduce in the individual experience—"interiorize"—the ancient forms of the archaic religion.[20] The cosmic dimension is replaced by the interior form of the experience. And the mystical "interiorization" or "spiritualization" of the archaic forms makes possible the immediacy and the all-consuming quality of the mystical experience, in such a way as to make possible an absolute form of world-negation. For the mystic, Being is the Nothing: and to the extent that he is conscious of Being *qua* being he lives on this side of the sacred Reality.

While there are grave religious differences between Oriental mysticism and the prophetic monotheistic religions of the Near East (Judaism, Zoroastrianism, Christianity, and Islam), the role of myth is parallel in their respective religious structures. It is now increasingly being recognized that the prophetic movement effected a revolutionary transformation of the ancient Israelite religion. Two generations ago Max Weber maintained that the substance of the prophetic message consisted in a sublimation of the traditional religion into ethical-eschatological absolutism.[21] Contemporary Old Testament scholarship tends to look upon the prophetic revolution as resting upon an eschatological religious foundation.[22] Apparently the pre-exilic prophetic oracles expect a cataclysmic judgment which would bring an end to Israel as a national community in history. It was just this judgment that brought an urgency to the prophetic message, thus making possible its absolute and seemingly utopian demand for righteousness. Although prophetic visions of the cosmic end of the world are lacking, we do find a religious attitude indifferent to man's pragmatic life in history—except insofar as this life is subject to God's judgment. The prophetic oracles are indifferent to family, state, and nature, for they are wholly grounded in Yahweh's coming acts—and to the obedience which these acts demand. It was this eschatological foundation of the

[20] See Mircea Eliade, *Yoga*, trans. Willard Trask (New York: Pantheon Books, 1958), especially pp. 293-358. Eliade minimizes the fact that the cosmic dimension of the archaic religion vanishes in the higher expressions of mysticism; one reason, perhaps, why he refuses to rank Tantrism below the classical forms of Indian mysticism.

[21] Max Weber, *Ancient Judaism*, trans. Hans Gerth and Don Martindale (Glencoe, Ill.: The Free Press, 1952), pp. 334-35.

[22] Cf. Thomas J. J. Altizer, "The Religious Foundations of Biblical Eschatology," *The Journal of Religion*, XXXIX (1959), 263-73.

prophetic movement which necessitated a transformation of the inherited "this-worldly" forms and beliefs of Israel's traditional religion.

The highest reaches of the prophetic spirit resist expression in the ancient religious forms. Despite the fact that the prophetic oracles echo the mythical and ritual forms of the ancient Near East, they transcend these forms insofar as they are directed to the dissolution of Israel's "historical" and this-worldly life. Ancient Israelite religion revolved about the worship of a god of power who would lead the people to triumph and prosperity in the world. But the prophetic movement inverted this messianic hope by proclaiming a final judgment upon Israel's historical existence.[23] Furthermore, as Weber has taught us, this transformation of the ancient religion was made possible by a "psychic economy" of the prophets which necessitated a suspension of the cultic and mythical expression of their experience.[24] Here, all the moral-religious energy of the prophet is vested in the demands which the End-time places upon the believer, without attention to the "meaning" of the End. Belief in the Day of the Lord is rather an inescapable consequence of an apprehension of Yahweh as the God of judgment who demands absolute righteousness. Rudolph Otto believed that the hidden mainspring of eschatology is ". . . the idea that righteousness is not possible in an earthly form of existence but only in the wholly other form of existence which God will give; . . . not possible in this age but only in a new age."[25] This accords well with Otto's belief that the holy is an utterly supermundane value and requires for its realization a supermundane existence.[26] Thus genuine eschatology invariably envisions a new creation which is coming in the near future.

The prophetic ideal is tantalizing insofar as it refuses to be compressed into ontological or mythical categories. It takes the eschatological ideal as its foundation, yet it holds back from all speculative

[23] Cf. Sigmund Mowinckel, *He That Cometh,* trans. G. W. Anderson (New York: Abingdon Cokesbury Press, 1956).

[24] Weber, *Ancient Judaism,* p. 317.

[25] Rudolph Otto, *The Kingdom of God and the Son of Man,* rev. ed., trans. Floyd Filson and Bertram Lee-Woolf (Boston: The Beacon Press, 1957), p. 49. Reprinted by permission.

[26] *Ibid.,* p. 59. Reprinted by permission.

or mythical conceptions of the End, not unlike early Buddhism. Nevertheless, the prophetic Day of the Lord is experienced as a "reality" whose realization will entail the destruction or reversal of the "reality" of the world. This truth is clearly apparent in the greatest of the prophetic books, Second Isaiah. All of Second Isaiah gives witness to the eschatological proclamation which is the foundation of its message; the prophet's promise of the coming redemption places in question the reality and value of all things. Yahweh's coming is intimately associated with a transformation of the world, with an End to reality as man has known it. Addressing the deaf and the blind, the Lord declares:

I will lay waste mountains and hills, and dry up all their herbage;
I will turn the rivers into islands, and dry up the pools.
And I will lead the blind in a way that they know not, in paths that they
    have not known I will guide them.
I will turn the darkness before them into light, the rough places into level
    ground. (42:15-16)

In the context of the announcement of the coming of Yahweh, the world itself loses its solidity. For the imminent advent of God is associated with an absolute form of world-reversal. A dominant theme of postbiblical Jewish mysticism conceives of the way to God as a reversal of the process of creation; similarly, the imagery of biblical eschatology sees the End as a re-enactment of the primordial acts of the Beginning. This motif is succinctly expressed in the Epistle of Barnabas: "Lo, I make the last things like the first" (6:13). The Lord of the End is the Lord of the Beginning, salvation is a re-enactment of creation, all things will pass away in order that all things may be made new. Accordingly, the Second Isaiah who can sing nature's praise of its Creator and Redeemer can no less passionately look forward to the coming End:

Lift up your eyes to the heavens, and look at the earth beneath; for the
    heavens will vanish like smoke, the earth will wear out like a garment,
and they who dwell in it will die like gnats;
but my salvation will be for ever, and my deliverance will never be ended.
    (51:6)

The triumphant message of Second Isaiah is that all things will soon be transformed, or will pass away, with the coming of God's acts of salvation. A disciple of Second Isaiah formulated this idea most clearly: "For behold, I create new heavens and a new earth; and the former shall not be remembered or come into mind" (65:17).

No longer is there any doubt that primitive Christianity falls under the category of eschatological religion. Its most significant difference from even the highest forms of Jewish eschatology, such as that of the Essenes, is that it has wholly sublimated the mythical-apocalyptic vision of the End into the rigor of an ethical-eschatological religious obedience; thus, in part, it represents a return to Israel's earlier prophetic faith, a faith which subordinated mythical vision to a demand for radical moral obedience. Primitive Christian eschatology, as reflected in the New Testament messages of Jesus and Paul, interiorized the underlying archaic mythical forms of eschatology, thus making possible a transformation of the cosmic dimension of archaic myth into an individual ethical-religious demand. Perhaps this truth is most obvious in the Sermon on the Mount, for Jesus' radical imperatives call his followers to a total obedience to God resting upon a rejection of the claims and values of "the world." Jesus confronts his disciples with an absolute religious demand which is grounded in the conviction that the Kingdom of God is now breaking into time, and thus already the world is passing away. Thus, to the believer, the values of the world are being reversed. And this reversal of worldly conditions makes possible the obedience which Jesus demands. Jesus repudiated his hearers' longing for apocalyptic signs and called them to an immediate ethical-religious response to the advent of the Kingdom. Consequently, the message of Jesus rests not upon a negation of myth, but upon an interiorization of the cosmic dimension of its archaic form.

The Christian is liberated from the world, not by an ascetic form of world-negation, but through having died and risen again with Christ. Albert Schweitzer makes this point about Paul:

He maintains the principle that a man should be as free as possible from earthly cares in order that his thoughts may be directed wholly to the Lord (I Cor. vii: 32); but the essential thing for him is the spiritual liberation from the earthly, not the outward. He therefore lays no special stress upon remoulding the daily life of the believer in consequence of the expectation of the imminent end of the world. . . . That is the meaning of the saying that those who have wives should be as though they have none, and those who weep as though they weep not, those who rejoice as though they rejoiced not, those who buy as though they possessed not, those who have to do with the world as though they did not use it (I Cor. vii:29-31). By substituting for renunciation of the earthly inner freedom from it, Paul cuts across the Early Christian world-negation in the same way as Buddha does with that of Brahmanism.[27]

Accordingly, the Christian has an inner freedom from the world by means of his life in the Christ who has come to end the world. Through his life in Christ, the Christian knows an absolute indifference to the world, an indifference created by a dying to the world; yet it is just this death to the world that makes possible a new freedom in Christ. Paul's eschatological faith revolves about a participation "even now" in the sacred time of the End, an End whose realization has already been inaugurated by the triumphant resurrection of Jesus. So Schweitzer says:

In the death of Jesus begins the cessation of the natural world, and in His resurrection the dawning of the supernatural world. This cosmic event translates itself in the created being, man, as a dying and rising again.[28]

And it is precisely through this dying and rising with Christ that the Christian receives God's forgiveness and knows the new reality of the Kingdom of God. Through suffering and dying with Christ, the Christian is made free from the world; this freedom from the world makes possible—demands—a new life of ethical obedience.

We must regard the prophetic movement in Israel, the reform of Zoroaster, primitive Christianity, and primitive Islam, as being so many varying forms of eschatological religion. These movements have major points in common: (1) they rest upon an expectation of the immediate end of the world, whether as world-transformation, world-reversal, or world-dissolution; (2) they subordinate myth-

---

[27] Albert Schweitzer, *The Mysticism of Paul the Apostle*, trans. William Montgomery (New York: The Macmillan Company, 1931), p. 312. Reprinted by permission of The Macmillan Company and A. & C. Black, Ltd.

[28] *Ibid.*, p. 23.

ical visions of the end to a radical form of moral obedience arising in response to the end; and (3) they call their followers out of their lives in history, and into a new interior reality of faith. However, we find a parallel phenomenon in the higher mystical religions of the Orient. What the eschatological believer knows as liberation from the world, the mystic knows as a loss of "consciousness," and a lack of awareness of the world. So likewise what the eschatological believer knows as a radical ethical obedience created by the dawning of the End, the mystic knows as a new contemplative life directed to the goal of the ontological dissolution of the world. The ultimate foundation of both mysticism and eschatology is a radically new participation in the sacred Reality which demands a dissolution or reversal of the reality of the world. Hence the mystic knows the world as the Nothing, for when the world becomes the Nothing, the sacred Reality becomes identified with reality itself. In a like manner, the eschatological believer knows the world as the old aeon, as doomed at any moment to pass away; for when the world has been destroyed, God will be all in all.

It would seem that the cosmic dimension of archaic myth has been negated in the higher religions, whether by means of mystical dissolution or eschatological reversal; and that, indeed, it is just this interiorization or sublimation of the cosmic dimension of myth that makes possible the higher expressions of religion. Now a new form of myth comes into existence, a form made possible by the new gulf which has arisen between man and the sacred, hence a form which by necessity cannot witness to the presence of the sacred in the world, and yet at the same time a form which reflects a new and immediate participation in the sacred. This higher form of myth is simply the vehicle for a new epiphany of the sacred, an epiphany which draws all things into itself. For the higher forms of religion are dedicated to the ultimate goal of identifying or realizing the sacred Reality as reality itself, therefore the deeper forms of myth direct themselves to a dissolution or reversal of everything which man knows and experiences, both as world and as self. By necessity, the cosmic dimension of myth must disappear if myth is to assume its highest function.

IV

This conception of myth and religion is based upon a scholarship and an understanding that may be peculiar to our time and religious situation. It is particularly striking that although the eschatological foundation of primitive Christianity is taken for granted today, it was not even discovered until the end of the nineteenth century—or at least not discovered by scholars; for eschatological faith was the guiding spirit of many sectarian and heretical movements in Christianity itself. Surely it is not accidental that the eschatological form of the early Christian Gospel came to be understood at a time when the foundations of Western civilization were seriously under attack. Nor did Oriental mysticism become a subject of serious Western interest and study until the nineteenth century. Is it an accident that Paul Deussen, one of the first scholars of the Vedanta, was an intimate friend of Nietzsche? Or that it was Schopenhauer who inspired so much interest in the mysticism of the East? Mysticism in the West (even from the time of the Greek and Hellenistic mystery cults) has always been a subterranean force, challenging the dominant currents of Western rationalism. And mysticism and eschatology have always revolted against the world-affirming consciousness of the West.

Modern literature and existentialism have made of the Nothing a reality which seems more real to us than Being. Heidegger, who believes that we are now living in the "Night of the World," conceives of Being itself as eschatological.[29] Sartre reverses the Cartesian tradition (with his declaration: "I am not, therefore I think"), and defines human consciousness (*pour-soi*) as nothingness.[30] And can one escape the spell of the Nothing who has been affected by the highest expressions of the modern theatre, the modern novel, and modern poetry—for a catalogue of the writers who have given a powerful witness to the Nothing would be little less than a list of

[29] Martin Heidegger, *Holzwege* (Frankfurt am Main: Vittorio Klostermann, 1950), p. 300. Cf. Thomas Langan, *The Meaning of Heidegger* (New York: Columbia University Press, 1959), pp. 143-65.

[30] Jean-Paul Sartre, *Being and Nothingness*, trans. Hazel Barnes (New York: Philosophical Library, 1956), pp. xlvii-lxix, 73-79, 617-28.

the great writers of our time. Neither our historical scholarship nor our religious understanding can be unaffected by such forces. Yet a recognition of this fact does not belie the nihilistic foundations of the higher expressions of religion. Modern thinkers of varying persuasions have become acutely aware of the problem of the meaning of myth and symbol. For we have been forced to employ myth and symbol at precisely those points where our ideas and concepts break down. Myth—the language of the religious symbol—is now seen to be the deepest and most authentic means for the expression of religious understanding and belief. Nevertheless, we can see that the highest expressions of myth are directed to the dissolution of the consciousness and the understanding which is a product of man's life in the world, of his life in Being.

Despite the fact that the modern mind cannot associate myth with truth, it must be forced to recognize that myth is the sole language of the deeper moments of religion. Kierkegaard initiated modern existentialism with his declaration that truth is subjectivity: *"An objective uncertainty held fast in an appropriation-process of the most passionate inwardness is the truth,* the highest truth attainable for an *existing* individual." [31] So it is that Kierkegaard provided a typically modern definition of faith as "precisely the contradiction between the infinite passion of the individual's inwardness and the objective uncertainty." [32] We must recognize—as Nietzsche taught us—that the world of faith is antithetical to everything which the modern world recognizes as truth and value. Modern man (Spengler's Faustian man or, more clearly, Nietzsche's Zarathustra, who says "Yes" to the earth) is radically world-affirming. Yet religious man engages in the deepest and most radical forms of world-negation. The man of faith is either without all consciousness of the world (mysticism), or he is so liberated from the world as to be absolutely indifferent to its forms and values (eschatology). Therefore while we must recognize the truth of Eliade's judgment that myth integrates man, the cosmos, and the sacred, we must

[31] Sören Kierkegaard, *Kierkegaard's Concluding Unscientific Postscript,* trans. David F. Swenson and Walter Lowrie (Princeton: Princeton University Press, 1941), p. 182. Reprinted by permission.
[32] *Ibid.* Reprinted by permission.

realize that this is true only of the initial or archaic moments of myth—or of those religious movements which attempt to reproduce the archaic ontology such as alchemy and Tantrism. The higher expressions of religion in East and West—always excepting Far Eastern mysticism—have evolved forms of myth directed to the End of the world, to the dissolution of man's life in Being.

Suggested Readings

Cassirer, Ernst, The Philosophy of Symbolic Forms, Vol. II, *Mythical Thinking*, trans. Ralph Manheim. New Haven: Yale University Press, 1955.

Eliade, Mircea, "Methodological Remarks on the Study of Religious Symbolism," *The History of Religions*, ed. Mircea Eliade and Joseph M. Kitagawa. Chicago: The University of Chicago Press, 1959, pp. 86-107.

Eliade, Mircea, *The Myth of the Eternal Return*, trans. Willard Trask. New York: Pantheon Books, 1954.

Eliade, Mircea, *Patterns in Comparative Religion*, trans. Rosemary Sheed. New York: Sheed and Ward, 1958, pp. 1-37, 367-465.

Johnson, F. Ernest, ed., *Religious Symbolism*. New York: Institute for Religious and Social Studies, 1955.

Leeuw, C. van der, *Religion in Essence and Manifestation*, trans. J. E. Turner. London: George Allen and Unwin, 1938, pp. 339-649.

Malinowski, Bronislaw, *Magic, Science and Religion*. New York: Doubleday and Co., 1954, pp. 93-148.

Otto, Rudolph, *The Kingdom of God and the Son of Man*, trans. Floyd Filson and Bertram Lee-Woolf. Boston: The Beacon Press, 1957, pp. 11-261.

Schweitzer, Albert, *The Mysticism of Paul the Apostle*, trans. William Montgomery. New York: Henry Holt and Company, 1931.

Wach, Joachim, *The Comparative Study of Religions*. New York: Columbia University Press, 1958, pp. 1-96.

Symbol and Myth

in Philosophy

Leroy E. Loemker

The science of the meaning and powers of symbols is as broad as human life itself, and is therefore a proper study for philosophy. *Homo loquens* is as distinctive a definition of man as *homo sapiens,* and far more inclusive of the breadth of experience with which philosophy is concerned. But man cannot speak without symbolizing. Since philosophy is concerned with the foundations or first principles of every field of human experience and life, every discussion of symbol and myth, whether in religion, poetry, science, or statecraft, is philosophical; it has only to search for these first principles or more general underlying assumptions, even though it may fail to reveal that ordered and coherent explication of all experience which philosophers have traditionally sought. It is the main contention of this paper, indeed, that the final justification of philosophy is its service to criticism, and that this requires an ordering and relating of the various roles of symbol in human life.

Though not all symbols are organized into linguistic systems, their philosophical significance may well be discussed within the context of language. Aristotle properly opens the *De Interpretatione* (which is itself the beginning of his studies in logic or the "Organon" of thought) with a definition of language. In doing this, he was the first Western philosopher (aside from Plato in a few remarks) to undertake a critical examination of the symbolic role of speech.

Spoken sounds [he says] are a showing of that which is in the soul as passions, and written signs are a showing [i.e., a symbolization] of spoken sounds. Just as all men do not have the same written signs, so all men do not have the same spoken signs. But the passions of the soul which these signs directly show forth [or symbolize] are the same in all men, as are also the things of which these are the analogical representations.[1]

Aristotle's remark might serve well as a gloss to the old Biblical myth of Babel, according to which the multiplication of tongues led to an abandonment of the common effort to express those passions of the soul in which men had agreed, but led also to the dispersion of peoples and the occupation of the inhabitable world. Aristotle's account puts language symbols in their proper context— "the passions of men" and the "things" to which these are conscious responses, that is, to the common internal and external experiences of men and their interplay upon each other. Symbols receive their meaning and their power from human awareness and the functions of mind in a social order.

The converse of this is, however, also true. We are all born into, and emerge as conscious beings within, an already existing world of signs, and develop as persons with growing freedom and self-determination only as we accept and submit to the various structured orders which constitute this world—eventually, as we become creative, adding new horizons and depths of meaning to the symbolic orders or languages within which our experience takes on form. Martin Heidegger recently defined the object of a philosophy of language (making use of the ambiguity in the German word *die Sprache,* which means at once the act of talking and the language or the system of organized symbols and rules by which one communicates) as "bringing speech as speech to speech," which we may perhaps render as "bringing language as speech [human communication] to self-expression." [2] Bruno Snell describes this omnipresent, decisive role of language in human experience by saying that it belongs to the nature of language to stand between the individual and the universal, between the subjective and the objective, between the arbitrary and the necessary.[3] Language is the emerging order and

---

[1] *De Interpretatione,* 16a.

[2] In a lecture on "Der Weg zur Sprache," in *Die Sprache,* published by the Bavarian Academy of Fine Arts (Darmstadt: Wissenschaftliche Buchgesellschaft, 1959), p. 94.

[3] Quoted by A. Püllman, "Vom sprachgebundenen Denken," *Frankfurter Allgemeine Zeitung,* June 27, 1959.

community of human experience within which each of us lives and
to which each may contribute.

I

Debates about the origin of language are as old as the
Sophists and Socrates, and the issue between nature and convention,
introduced by Protagoras, is still unresolved. Even today, the discussion of language and symbolic form is complicated by the variety of philosophical approaches made to it by the founders of
modern semantics. For example, Peirce treats the symbolic relationships realistically so that reality becomes a flowing and continuous
structure of social symbolization; Cassirer's Neo-Kantianism is revealed by his treating the internal dynamic of symbolism in history
under the general title of *Man;* Whitehead includes the symbolic
process in a general objective order of events; recent positivists
undertake a narrow phenomenalistic approach to the verification or
application of symbolic structures.[4] Rather than try to differentiate
these varied philosophies, we shall proceed to basic definitions and
attempt to explicate a general area of agreement. Even here, however, usage is confused, and our definitions must be set up somewhat arbitrarily.

A *sign,* we may say, is any natural object or event, simple or complex, which leads some sentient being, becoming aware of it, to
respond to a wider situation of which the sign is a part or an effect
(or cause). Thus two events naturally related become the sign and
the thing signified (*signatum*) only when one serves as stimulus to a
living, sentient being to respond to the other. Thus thunder is a
sign of rain, and rain a sign of physical discomfort, or perhaps, in
certain situations, of a restful day at home. The flash of the white
underside of a deer's tail alerts his companions and poises them for
flight. Such a sign, when it evokes specific action as a response, may
be called a *signal.* The white flash of a tail evokes the response of

---

[4] See particularly the essay on "Logic as Semiotic: The Theory of Signs," in
The Philosophy of Peirce: Selected Writings, ed. Justus Buchler (New York:
Harcourt, Brace & World, Inc., 1940), pp. 98-119; Ernst Cassirer, *An Essay on
Man* (New York: Doubleday and Co., 1953); Alfred North Whitehead, *Symbolism,
Its Meaning and Effect* (New York: The Macmillan Company, 1927).

running or flight; in a loose sense one may say that this is what it means to the deer.

A *symbol* is the special case of a sign in which there is involved between sign and signatum, in addition to this functional correspondence, a conscious or conceptualized reference. If the white flash of tail means not merely the evocation of an impulse to run, but an imperative, "Run!"—a consciously conceived imputation to the sign of its meaning—then the sign becomes a symbol. Symbols may be natural or arbitrarily chosen, but they involve the signification of things which can be conceptually related to them, whether the things signified be commands, facts, theories, or felt states of consciousness. There is always possible a conscious reference from symbol to the thing symbolized, even though the effect of symbols may not be primarily conceptual.

A symbol, then, has conscious meaning. It is therefore on the level of symbols that man's distinctive capacities and powers operate. Symbols may still have a natural basis for their correspondence to what is symbolized; thus, sense qualities may symbolize physical processes (light waves of a particular frequency, and so on) or neurological fields, and certain colors or sounds may also refer naturally to emotional or motor attitudes with which they are causally connected. These latter significations are sometimes expressed metaphorically in such common phrases as "feeling blue" and "seeing red." But the symbols which have extended human experience most widely are arbitrary (at least in part), and subject to human alteration, manipulation, organization, and expansion.

A *language* is a more or less complex set of symbols, oral or written, together with a set of rules governing their structural combination and use in communication. In ordinary natural languages these rules of grammar are somewhat conventional and established by custom. Yet they conform to logical requirements as well since they are intended to cover adequately the entire area of experience, or in the case of more esoteric languages, some special area of experience. Without some rational structure, intelligent communication would be impossible.

The scope of languages is, however, wider than the "natural" languages. Edward Kasner, one of America's most distinguished mathematicians, used to say that there are only two universal languages—

mathematics and music. This is an ambiguous statement. On the one hand, it may mean that these are universal languages in the sense that all men—that is, all men who are literate in these languages—can use them in communication with each other; that in some way mathematics and music are forms of communication which transcend the confusion of tongues and the resulting dispersion of the peoples. On the other hand, it may mean that these two languages are capable, as others are not, of communicating all of the experiences of men; that what can be *thought* (and what cannot?) can be communicated mathematically, and what can be *felt* (and again, what cannot?) can be communicated in music. It was Galileo who said that the language of nature is written in mathematical symbols, and his contemporary, Kepler, who said that God geometrizes, and both Kepler and Galileo were deeply involved in working out the theory of harmony to which music has until recent times adhered.

Both claims of universality can be challenged, of course, for it is obvious that in these days mathematicians speak and write for mathematicians; while Leibniz's dream of a universal calculus, which should exhaust the realm of truth, is still only a dream. And modern musicians are widely suspected, like poets, of composing only for musicians (or poets). Moreover, one who listens to a program of Balinese gamelan music, or for that matter, to a cantor singing the old hymns of the Jews with their affinities with the rhythms of Hebrew verse, must acknowledge that the language of music is relative to group and tradition, as is every language under the sun. Mathematics is too abstract to communicate the concrete, a role essential to universal speech. It is noteworthy, however, that people of widely differing cultures quickly learn to "listen to" or to "hear" (in a musical sense) the musical utterances of others—the ecstatic song of Greek chorus, the lamentation of the Jewish cantor, the gamelan orchestra's intricate surface of thin but pure melody.

Yet it is true, not only that mathematics and music are both languages, but that they are abstract languages whose symbolic structures lack a direct reference to a perceived world. Mathematics is formal; its relations are its own, though its methods and conclusions may find a host of useful applications in the understanding of the physical or even the mental world. And for the most expressive music a "program" is irrelevant; there is no specific reference to events or relations in nature or human affairs. Nevertheless both music and mathematics have a symbolic content and a structure or formal pattern of relations into which that symbolic content is organized. But the symbolic reference of the two is different. For want of better terms, the symbols of mathematics may be called conceptual, those of music, evocative. The former operate on the level of man's intellect; the latter evoke responses lying deeper in the nature of the personality.

II

Symbols serve many purposes, but their primary function is, as we have said, to symbolize; that is, to *represent*, or *express* (it is to Leibniz that we owe these two equivalent terms) something particular (a thing, an act, a relation, a quality, or a person) or a universal or class of things. This representative function deserves somewhat closer attention. Symbols may express things present or things absent, and of the latter, things past and things thought of as future. They may also represent things nonexistent and things whose existence is impossible. They may be used to discover things hitherto unknown. Thus symbols serve man in the role of memory and anticipation as well as present recognition; and anticipation may become prediction if the symbol contains relational terms which previous experience has shown to have a high degree of certitude. The causal relation is of primary importance in this respect.

Symbols may be *simple* or *compound*. The basic compound symbol in natural language is the sentence, or, translated into logical terms, the proposition. According to traditional logic, *terms* or *names* (categorematic words) have a reference or denotation, but are neither true nor false. Combined with certain "syncategorematic" words, however (words like *is* in its various forms, *all, some, is not, or, and,* etc.), they become claimants of truth or falsehood. The term "purple cow" involves no claim of truth or falsehood, but combined with the copula "to be" and the quantifier "some" it becomes "Some cows are purple" and becomes a truth claim. It was the general conclusion of the Ockhamistic logic that in any categorical sentence or proposition, the categorematic terms provide the reference to the objects known, while the syncategorematic terms have no denotation or reference to objects but are provided by the thinking mind. This view ran contrary to an established Scholastic position which held that sentences are abstractions from substantial composites—substances and their properties and relations and motion—so that the compound symbolic assertion immediately contains the very essence or form of the objective situation represented. There is no mediation through a "suppositive" or substantival reference.

This old problem is recalled here because the Ockhamistic interpretation lies at the root of a modern tendency to hold that the relations in knowledge must be supplied by the knowing mind, and that only substantive, qualitative, and process terms stand for objects known. Thus the seeds of modern subjectivism were planted early, to mature in a variety of opinions including Locke's, Hume's, Kant's, and that of modern positivism in general. At the turn of the last century, however, there was a widespread return to a more realistic conception of objective reference and to theories of knowledge, whether idealistic, phenomenological, or neorealistic, which affirmed a direct reference, not only of the content terms, but of the connectives, to a relational or structured pattern of existence, so that there is some real identity of structure binding linguistic utterance to objective fact, or in general, language to reality.

We shall refer to this epistemological position as *isomorphism,* meaning by this term to assert the identity, complete or partial, of the form of a complex symbol with the form of the object it symbolizes. When developed into a metaphysics, isomorphic interpretations may differ in being idealistic or realistic, depending upon whether they regard the cumulative total of forms thus symbolized as fundamentally a whole, and this a mental whole, or whether they regard the symbolic process as penetrating ever more deeply, as experience increases and analysis and synthesis of symbols move further and further from the particular and discrete to the general and mutually dependent, into a real other world about which neither wholeness nor mindlikeness can be asserted. Charles Saunders Peirce seems to have resolved these two positions by recognizing the essential mental, yet ever incomplete, form of symbol and referent and identifying it immediately with the real order of experience engendering and harmonizing the process which is the world.

There has been since the days of Leibniz a dream of perfecting a system of symbols to represent and to operate with all possible experience, but also to present a formally self-consistent implicative system, so that, given an adequate set of primary symbols, the axioms which determine their relationships, and the rules of logical procedure, all truth could be determined and established on a distinct and adequate basis. Whether this is the business of theoretical grammar, of logic (defined by Peirce as semiotic or the science of signs), or of mathematics is not yet clear; perhaps the issue is largely a linguistic one. In any case the dream has not yet been actualized, nor has it yet been proved possible. Indeed, it would seem to be proved both impossible (by Gödel) and undesirable if freedom and an open indeterminate future are practical necessities of life. Mathematics still seems to provide the simplest and most useful special cases of such symbolic systematizations of fields of thought.

III

Symbols and symbolic systems serve many purposes. This may be seen by enumerating some of the common types of such systems. One may, as has already been suggested in part, distinguish three different types of symbolic reference, following Aristotle's three divisions of the field of human experience: the theoretical or logical, in which the symbolic relation aims at knowledge; the practical, in which the symbol means action; and the poetical or aesthetic, in which the symbol means a complex inward state of the soul, an emotional attitude or sentiment.

Among the types of logical or intellectual symbolic structures can be named sentences, whether categorical, hypothetical, or disjunctive; pictures insofar as they are representative; formulas; laws; tables; graphs; maps; schedules; theories; models; systems. Among the practical symbolic forms are commands; instructions; plans; operational models; rites; ideals; Utopias. Among the aesthetic and evocative symbolic forms may be listed selected natural or artificially combined organizations of colors, shapes, tones, either spatially or temporally structured or both; the visual arts, poetry and music, the dance. That symbolic forms do not belong simply to one of the three types is shown by the various forms of poetry, myths, architecture, and other arts.

We may now proceed to enumerate some of the more obvious mixed uses of symbolic systems. They are the keys to processes of learning, to effective action, and to intrinsic human values.

(1) They serve to *remember*—not merely to recall, but to conserve economically what has been learned until it is needed. The once highly respected science of mnemonics was based upon the association of symbols. In the solution of a complex problem in mathematics an equation covering several pages of text may be carried forward by a single symbol until the time arrives for its particular internal formulations to be used. In geometry a single term such as *triangle* holds in suspension a very complex system of logically dependent theorems and corollaries from which any one relation may be drawn when it is needed.

(2) Thus many symbols (among them the most important) are clues or even guides to operations. To one familiar with them they become commands to act, and directions for action. What is, for thought, a relation of cause to effect may become, for action, the relation of means to ends; thus the distinction between theoretical and practical symbols is not a sharp one. The traffic sign, "Limit 30 miles" is informational, but it moves many a foot off the accelerator, and commands, or advises, looking around for a policeman. The fraction line in arithmetic stands both for a kind of quantified relation and for an operation. And Leibniz's symbols for the differential and integral calculus are preferred to Newton's fluxional notation because of their operational suggestiveness; in a sense, the symbols themselves contain the solutions. In ordinary life operational symbols are easy to find—the instructions on do-it-yourself kits, dressmaking patterns, symbolic keys for dance steps, traffic lights and highway signs, among many.

(3) The use of cognitive or denotative symbols in discovery is a further extension of their value. Discovery may be narrowly empirical and accidental, but it may be, and in science often is, a process of inference in which the symbolic structure is extended, by

some logically justifiable process of conjecture, interpolation, or extrapolation, beyond that part abstracted from the given datum, however structured. For symbolic systems are selective; they do not express all that is given but only the aspects and relations considered important for the purpose at hand; hence there is always an aspect of hazard and adventure in the symbols from which hypotheses are built. The periodic table of chemical elements has proved to have such discovery value of a high degree of accuracy; so do the benzene ring of Kekule and the model of an atom; indeed, several different models of atoms have each had value in predicting and discovery. The adventure of knowledge is thus largely the abstracting of the "right" or needed structures from a given problem situation—the selection of those skeletal aspects, so to speak, and those rules of combination which offer the greatest promise for a symbolic extension to the solution of new problems.

(4) A further extension of the intellectual use of symbols is presented in logic. Here symbolism is designed to aid in the process of critical thinking itself—a formalization of inference, necessary and contingent logical dependence, existential reference, and all the other relations of logic, designed to reduce thinking itself to signs and rules of calculation. One needs to keep in mind, of course, that this mathematico-mechanistic reduction of thought is an abstract one which omits all the extra-logical psychological factors affecting a thinker, and therefore cannot serve as an adequate guide, *in concreto,* to human reasoning.

(5) Symbols thus, by their very selective nature, readily take on a normative role; being abstract, they tend to contain only that aspect of the referent which the selecting and symbolizing agent considers important or useful. In the simplest meaning of the term, they are ideal and embody a meaning of what is of *value* or *ought to be.*

The magical use of symbols is a natural, but illogical, development of this normative, valuative function; we are all disposed to fall into it. Magic imputes to the symbol itself an operative force for good or ill, apart from its basic function as a symbol. Thus we hang the flag in certain prescribed ways with the feeling that to do otherwise would be bad, and we are taught to "pledge allegiance" to it. The token of the patron saint of travellers has become for many a magical protection from accident. We use words as if they had magical attributes. The confusion of magic with religion is widespread. In all these cases, magic ignores the limitations imposed on more or less arbitrary symbols by their symbolic character. From a logical viewpoint, the magical use of symbols is therefore something to be exorcised, to be cancelled out, but from a human point of view magic is ineradicable.

(6) A most important role of symbols is that of making possible communication and cooperation. It is essential to symbols to serve a social purpose. They are used by someone to express some meaning to someone. Even a private symbol, such as a thread tied around my finger to remind myself of some task, is a communication by myself of eight in the morning to myself of three in the afternoon. To *communicate* is to accept a common set of symbols and a common set of conventions for their use, in order that a meaning, after being translated into this symbolic language by one person may be inferred from it, by the same rules, by another person. *Cooperation* takes places when a common plan or ideal or operational model is accepted and resolved upon through communication by two or more persons, or when two or more persons through communication establish a common purpose and then determine the place of the separate acts of each in a common resultant action toward this common purpose. *Communion* involves the adoption, by a group, of common intellectual symbols and the execution of common ritual acts in the conservation of common recognized values. And a community is the permanent social state sustained by a more or less systematic whole of such common symbolic patterns, cognitive, imperative, evocative, and operative. These take the form of myths, laws and customs, and rites.

The cognitive role of symbols is thus continuous with their non-rational role, whether sacramental, ritualistic, or in some other way evocative of the emotional attitudes of satisfaction or dissatisfaction, commitment or rejection. The distinction between theoretical, practical, and evocative symbols cannot be drawn sharply. Indeed, practical and evocative symbols can be resolved by language into intellectual symbols which can be analyzed, criticized, and improved. Thus the rather fatuous polysyllabic street signs often used to require city dwellers to curb their dogs may well be subjected to intellectual criticism by judging them according to other symbolic norms to which they may or may not conform—symbols of legibility (perhaps a standard model of an easily readable type), of intelligibility (perhaps a standard world list of basic English), of perceptibility (a standard color contrast for highest distinctness), or of aesthetic taste (an ideal of simple, clear English, or an ideal of harmonic form applied to the sign and its environment). Or, more simply, the efficacy of the red light commanding traffic to stop may be subject to criticism in terms of a physiological table or scale of color perception. And while the actual red cannot be communicated, it can be symbolized in a variety of structures which make communication about *red* possible. This is an important point. Many human experiences may be incommunicable, but few are so in the sense that discourse about them is impossible in terms of the suitable symbolic systems into which they and their situations can be translated.

IV

We have several times alluded to a further function of symbols which falls within the field of aesthetics, and contrasts rather sharply with the representation of an objective state. This is their role in giving immediate expression to, or (if it is absent) evoking immediately, a subjective or inward state of the person to whom the symbol is presented. What is involved in this expression and evocation may be not merely simple feelings, but more abiding moods, dispositions of the person, tensions, and harmonies. Susanne K. Langer has discussed this role of symbols in *Philosophy in a New Key*. Feelings, she says, have definite forms which become "progressively articulated," and the function of art is to evoke and to further this growing articulation.[5] Moreover, as feelings are articulated, they develop into habitual dispositions or attitudes which may be called personal value-attitudes or commitments. The patterns of the arts have significance insofar as they "logically resemble," intensify, and articulate these emotive structures, commitments, readinesses to act. They may have cognitive representative roles as well;

[5] Susanne K. Langer, *Philosophy in a New Key* (Baltimore: Penguin Books, 1948), pp. 75, 163-66, 195-99.

paintings or drawings may be pictures, the symbolic pattern of a poem may require deciphering like a cryptogram, and music may have an obvious or concealed program. But the distinctive function of art is the significant expression and intensified evocation of a personal value inclination (or frustration).

Efforts have been made to study analytically the immediate intuitive relationship between the sensory components of art and feelings. Many years ago the Gestaltists pointed out the intimately felt coordinations of sensations and the feelings which the arts involve—the warmth and coldness of colors, the lightness and darkness of tones, the anger and serenity of lines, atonalities, and harmonies. Extensive analysis would reveal multitudes of possible structural coordinates possible in a work of art. But of course composition is not accumulation, and evocative force or significance increases greatly as the work of art achieves some organic unity of these forms and qualities, so that the deeper needs and commitments of man may find expression through the perceived art work.

The symbolic role of art in evoking the religious attitude has been widely discussed. Rudolph Otto's discussion has been influential.[6] The a-rational component of religious experience—the experience of the "numinous" as *mysterium tremendum et fascinosum* —is expressed most effectively in the form of the sublime, not merely in architecture but in ritual gesture, poetry, and song. In this process the elementary magical component of religion is "ennobled and illumined," so that religion is purified and made aware of itself through the dynamic of the great throbbing rhythms and the sweep (*Schwingungen*) of its great expressions. Otto finds this transformed magical quality particularly in the Taoist visual art of China. Secondary manifestations of the numinous are silence and darkness (Western religious art has sometimes mastered these), and emptiness or an extensive void (whose religious use is known only in the East).

Music is that art *par excellence* in which the expressive power of the tonal patterns evoke deepest personal harmonies and conflicts, devotions and insights, experiences which lie beneath the logic of ordinary language and analysis.

[6] Rudolph Otto, *The Idea of the Holy*, rev. ed., trans. J. W. Harvey (New York: Oxford University Press, 1950), pp. 65-71.

The interesting question of whether all art, insofar as it is successful, expresses the religious attitude, or whether there are effective aesthetic expressions of other basic if not "ultimate" human attitudes is one which cannot be discussed here. The former view has been urged on different grounds by many writers, including Richard Wagner and Jacques Maritain; Paul Tillich is a contemporary thinker who advocates the latter position. Yet it may be added that there is a similarity between play, art, and religion which is worth pondering. In all three there is symbolism, a doing something which stands for something, but with a merging, in the mind, or the reality with the symbol; the act itself is of supreme importance. In all three there is thus an element of magic inherent in the symbol and its power, and in all there is a total surrender of the person, for the time being, to the symbol and this "wholly other" power.

V

Myth is a primary but complex art form, "the father of poetry," whose genesis is religious and which is therefore clothed in the sense of the numinous. A myth is a story which offers answers —sometimes intellectual answers (as in the case of aetiological myths), but answers athrob with the sense of the sacred—to the ultimate questions of the group—questions which are matters of life, not merely of understanding.

Myth is not the only symbolic form in religion; in fact it overlaps ritual and sacrament. All three participate in the magical and the holy. The speech of myth is evocative; to the mythmaker it reveals the deity in the fulness of his holy power. To modern man it may still speak in the evocative illumining sense, but only if it is one of the truly great utterances concerning man's need and destiny. On the other hand, as Walter Otto has pointed out, its evocative power may be dangerous and unwholesome.[7] Myths do not arise from man's unconscious, and only secondarily speak to it. Being the work of the imagination and therefore of the intelligence of man operating within the limits of tradition and of what is

[7] Walter Otto, *Theophania, Der Geist der altgriechischen Religion* (Hamburg: Rohwalt, 1956), pp. 19-21, 23.

naïvely perceived, myth must enter into a dialectic with the moral imperatives which also are a part of the religious attitude. It cannot penetrate beyond the reach of the understanding, or at least of the imagination, that intellectual power which, Bacon tells us, mediates between sense and reason, between reason and human use. Myths, by their nature, may embody the ultimate intuitions and insights of a thoughtful people, but they are not by this fact lifted beyond the range of logical analysis and criticism.

The Platonic use of myths is a philosophical and pedagogical one. The myths in the Platonic dialogues retain the evocative power of great poetry, but have lost the magic of religious faith, though most of them were clearly religious in origin. No single principle governed Plato's use of them. The myth of Er (*Republic,* X) was an eschatological myth, but Plato's application of it was to the problem of moral self-determination in the daily decisions of life; the poetic grandeur of the story must have been designed chiefly for pedagogical reasons, not merely to persuade but to move the youth to good choices. Yet it contains components, such as the great cosmology, which were expressible by the science of Plato's time. The creation myth in the *Timaeus* is essentially metaphysical, not in an allegorical sense but in a sense which Whitehead could translate directly into a phenomenological philosophy. The myth of the soul in the *Phaedrus* does attempt to carry the hearer's perceptions beyond conceptual analysis, to show the mystical character of man's grasp of the Good which unifies and gives life to the Ideas but lies beyond them. The philosophic use of myths thus gives them the character of parable or allegory, but with direct references to the human situation and thus with moral and educational, as well as constructive philosophical, intent.

For the goal of intellectual clarity, magic is to be exorcised. It pervades the symbolism of man living in what Maritain calls "the darkness of imagination," from the level of mere word magic to that of elaborate rituals and creeds (*symbols,* we call these in the Christian tradition).[8] It is perhaps for this reason that Bergson discusses myth as a manifestation of static religions and does not admit it, except as a kind of preparatory phase, to the dynamic

[8] Jacques Maritain, *Ransoming the Time* (New York: Charles Scribner's Sons, 1941), pp. 227-36.

religion of the spirit.[9] What keeps magic from becoming applied science is its indifference to careful observation and its outreach for a rationally illegitimate power. Magic belongs, as Maritain says, to a dream era, not a logical era. Science advances by treating signs as logical and rejecting any evocative effect they may have—and they do have this—on the mind of the scientist. A magical sign, on the other hand, ascribes to the symbol not merely a denotation but an efficient causal power.[10]

All religious symbolism, including, in addition to myths, religious rites, creeds, and sacraments, is thus involved in the dialectic or "alternation" between the rational and the irrational in religion, though the distinct forms vary in the degree to which they mix the objective, cognitive function with the nonrational evocative role of the symbol.

VI

The philosophical issues concerning symbols center in the role, integral or centrifugal, which they play in the life of man and in his culture. Is the relation which is possible between different symbolic structures—among which we have discussed here the logical, the aesthetic, and the religious—one merely of external alternation, or is there an inclusive and coherent pattern of the whole? (We have not considered such questions as the politico-social role of ideals, plans of action, commands or laws, Utopias, and other symbols of this nature.) Is there a direction toward unity and what are its conditions? One answer is that of Spranger and others who have set up a typology of men, each type having one dominant interest which determines the role of the rest. Tillich and others have similarly set up a typology of cultures and dealt with their dynamic interrelations. Cassirer proposes that as man progresses in his use of symbols from the mythical and magical to the scientific, this use carries him to increasing freedom. Malraux, on the other hand, seems to suggest, on the basis of the symbolic role of art, that the

[9] Henri Bergson, *The Two Sources of Religion and Morality* (Garden City: Doubleday and Co., 1954), pp. 107-11.

[10] Maritain, *op. cit.*, p. 226.

path is toward increasing solitariness and frustration. The religious person may say, "By grace alone," but how much does this "alone," this assertion of the exclusive worth of the religious, exclude? It is a claim made by Catholic humanists, by Puritan activists, by saints and mystics, and by men of rugged, uninspired commitment; and by all of these with truth.

One answer philosophy must sustain. It may justly admit that one mystic vision is worth a hundred Aquinases, or that a profoundly revealing myth (though many myths are not profound, nor revealing, but only playful, grotesque, or informative) may be worth volumes on the nature and destiny of man. But it must also insist, in all of these a-rational roles of symbols, on the possibility and the necessity of criticism and communication. Evocative symbols are at the heart of our life, and this heart cannot be moved merely by logic. But the power of myths lies in their expressive and evocative nature and in their human compulsiveness; they do not *per se* contain a guarantee of their own truth. Mystic and artist as well as moralist have talked about their experiences, ineffable though these may be, and this linguistic symbolization of the symbolic role itself makes criticism possible, and with it the application of norms of validity, maturity, fruitfulness, and "reality" or truth. This is the role of philosophy.

Perhaps philosophy can go still further in this rational discourse, and play a constructive or speculative role. Such construction cannot create the deep experiences of life nor evoke their full spiritual expression, any more than a physical definition can reproduce, or even define, the sensation of color. But all experiences must receive conceptual interpretation if there are to be possibilities of correction. The *mysterium tremendum et fascinosum* has bred holy but devastating wars; something very like it has swept the world into disaster recently, and may do so again. And a godly righteousness, impervious to criticism, may bedevil a people and commit it to ignorance and blind loyalty to what is proclaimed as the voice of God. We must consider the spirits, and the symbols, whether they be of God. The constructive role of philosophy may even be defined through a norm. The full development of personality is made possible only when the logical and the a-logical evocative and dynamic roles of the symbolic systems within which the person develops, reinforce and support each other; when scientific criticism can examine the cultural myths without destroying their valid poetic power; when human capabilities develop harmoniously through the reasonably related and structured symbolic orders which communicate meaning and value. Hence when the social agencies of communication and education, however complex, are brought to a mutual harmony and reinforcement of the symbolic orders which they use, the conditions are established for free personal development which is at once intelligent, imaginative, and socially beneficent. The problem is to find symbols which can together evoke both discrimination and adventure, both creativity and order, both moral discretion and poetic vision. An impossible ideal, certainly, but one of those ought-to-be-yet-cannot-be ideals which have always haunted the horizons of morality and given it direction.

Maritain is thus right, it seems, in reaffirming a role of reason broader than that of science, but to which the scientific contributes essential information and critical attitudes. This higher use is philosophy. Religious experience may rise above it; so may poetry, music, and the other consummatory experiences of man. Life is indeed more than reason. But reason is never, as extreme existentialists have claimed, completely irrelevant. If it were, the myth of Babel would forever condemn men to failure in their efforts to understand and to cooperate with each other. The isolation of different groups and their diverging traditions would remain invincible, and we should never, except superficially, be able to join in mutual respect and common creative purpose.

Suggested Readings

Cassirer, E., *An Essay on Man*. Garden City: Doubleday and Company, Inc., 1953. (Anchor Books A3).

Langer, Susanne K., *Philosophy in a New Key*. New York: Penguin Books, Inc., 1948. (Pelican, P25).

Maritain, Jacques, *Ransoming the Time*. New York: Charles Scribner's Sons, 1941. Chapter IX, pp. 217-54.

Peirce, Charles Saunders, "Logic as Semiotic: The Theory of Signs" in J. Buchler, *Philosophical Writings of Peirce*. New York: Dover Books,

1955, pp. 98-119. See also the letter to Lady Welby, March 14, 1909, in *Values in a Universe of Chance,* ed. P. P. Wiener. Garden City: Doubleday, 1958, pp. 412-22. (Anchor 126).

Whitehead, A. N., *Symbolism, Its Meaning and Effect.* New York: The Macmillan Company, 1927.

The Literary Uses of

Myth and Symbol

Ward Pafford

I

There are few areas of critical speculation more baffling and recalcitrant than the one harboring myth and symbol. Anthropology, linguistics, psychology, philosophy, and literary criticism have pursued the subject with dubious success. It therefore seems sensible to attempt an exploration of the notoriously elusive aspects of myth and symbol in literature by trusting a fresh and basic approach rather than the complex apparatuses previously devised.

A useful directive is the relative position of myth and symbol within religion. These two troublesome phenomena have no pretension of absoluteness like that of private religious experience or a comprehensive or institutional critique. Private religious experience points only toward union with God; criticism points in a single direction, but precisely opposite, toward rational apprehension. Within this framework, myth and symbol point toward both the ineffable and the tangible. They are of great importance in the religious concern, for the moment the religious man turns his face away from God and outward toward other men or inward toward his own being, he creates myth and symbol in the attempt to embody—not yet to explain, but to show—something of the nature of his experience with God. Theology and ecclesiasticism in their turn become increasingly sophisticated and, perhaps, remote refinements upon what was just myth and symbol.

Whereas for religion myth and symbol may be relative in function and value, these devices for the poet as poet (to use the term as broadly as Aristotle though not so broadly as Shelley in his "Defence of Poetry") are absolute. They are for him as artist, and in extreme "romantic" cases as man, a unique order of reality having ultimate value. Such a view makes two fundamental assumptions about poetry: one, that the poem is an autonomous system, although it may look like an imitation of objective reality or a projection or expression of subjective experience; second, that the poem contains essentially a myth or symbol more important for the poet than the thing represented, whether objective or subjective. The latter notion suggests a radical view of the work of art as a relatively pure element, useful mainly for separating works of art from non-art. For those who find it possible to accept such an attitude, however, the poetic use of symbol is distinctive and may form, on occasion, an absolute value.

Poetry may be defined (according to the ancients) as a "making" through the medium of language, an imaginative creativity involving a kind of imitation. Hence a poem cannot be the "real thing," even though some—especially the poet himself if he is serious— may value it far more highly then "reality." Moreover, if poetry is a making, then one assumes that form is involved which differentiates it from either abstraction or chaos. Also, insofar as a poem is not a pure creation but a kind of imitation, it must make symbolic reference to things: visions, states of mind, feelings, as well as so-called objective phenomena. The essential thing about poetry is that it points in a contrived and symbolic way in two directions simultaneously: toward an ideal order available only through the imagination and toward the stuff of material experience. It is a dual effort struggling to become a single one, two-faced like Janus. This process or conflict is always present in the poem, whether described in the classical terms of imitation, in the romantic terms of appearance and reality, or according to an arbitrary impersonal formula like that of T. S. Eliot in modern times, which questions whether there is any reality at all beyond the self. Poetry demands by the very process of its creation, a transfiguration, but only a partial one, since it can never forsake or hide its mundane roots. Thus it is always impure.

Other devices which are the common ingredients of poetry are all fundamentally metaphorical—they catch up and incorporate the features of one thing under the guise of another. They are all, as an uncouth Platonist might put it, a pack of lies; or, in the Aristotelian view, vehicles of truth that possess certain advantages over history and science, but only for one willing to view truth itself as multi-dimensional and, along with this primary pluralism, to look forward with satisfaction to the strangely monistic, though externally various, achievement of metaphor.

Those parts of speech normally employed in the poem for strictly logical purposes—conjunctions, prepositions, articles, and the like —as well as general or abstract words which make no immediate and vital connection with sense experience, are signs. When Milton, for example, refers to "Things unattempted yet in Prose or Rhime," he is employing essentially this kind of sign language. This is plainly a different expression from his "Dove-like satst brooding on the vast Abyss/And mads't it pregnant. . . ." In comparison, the sign appears to be a product of mechanical and deliberate maneuvering and possesses little intrinsic value or interest. It may point in two directions, but significantly in only one—back to the data for which it stands. Hence it is falsely metaphorical. It attracts no lively response from eye or ear, however useful it may be in conceptual manipulation. As far as imaginative literature is concerned, language as pure sign is of little higher value than the conventions of punctuation inserted as mechanical means of guidance.

Image is the most elemental form of true metaphor, and we recognize it at once as such. It always results from an interest in selecting, in some degree intuitively, an appropriate agent for data from nature and sensory experience to produce an invariably concrete image, like Milton's brooding dove. It has been claimed for centuries, of course, that the image-making faculty is the distinguishing mark of the poetic mind, and this view may hold true regardless of shifts in fashion, from a prosy discursive rendering of feeling, to the extravagances of esoteric symbolism, and back again. But the essential characteristic of the image—its intrinsic sensuous appeal—gives it its superiority (with respect to poetic values) to the sign. Like the sign, it points in only one direction, but to nature rather than to the fabrications of abstract reason.

The symbol is immediately recognized as an image of special significance, but never as merely a sign. The albatross in Coleridge's great ballad of crime and punishment or Hawthorne's scarlet letter are, for nearly all readers, images which quickly acquire status as symbols when their uses are explored. The symbol invariably possesses the sensuous quality of the image that marks its relation to the concrete and thus has intrinsic value as object. But it is different from the image in that, though attractive in itself, it becomes imbued with an abstract significance, often of great power, as it points away from its referents. And as the image seems to be predominantly sensuous and concrete, so the symbol seems to be weighted in the direction of the non-finite. As neither sign nor image can do, it acts as intermediary between the indefinite and the definite and is, so to speak, charged in both directions. Its complexity may also be suggested by noting the frequent use of multiple images so related that the symbol dominating the context may acquire an unusual richness and depth; the symbolic sensual world abandoned by Yeats' old man in favor of Byzantium, for instance. Tennyson's Lancelot (in "The Lady of Shalott") is another impressive, though rather garish, example.

Myth differs from symbol essentially in its representation of a supermundane order which the symbol may imply without much, if any, elaboration. And just as the symbol may be enriched by supporting and clustered images, so may the myth acquire depth and coherence by a context of harmonious symbols, with imagery present for embellishment and incidental clarification. The differences here are again largely in degree, with myth usually the more elaborate construction, most often represented in literature in the form of narrative (epic, drama, novel). The notion that myth as employed in literature refers to an origin in the hallowed mists of ancient time is more an historical observation of well-known or discoverable mythological figures or narratives rather than a definition, and it somewhat obscures the perennial vitality of myth-making instincts. Richard Chase convincingly argues that myth construction in modern literature is found whenever an order beyond that of space-time needs to be suggested,[1] though upon strict consideration a confusion in his distinction between the function of myth and symbol may appear.

At whatever level or stage the metaphorical impulse occurs, myth is likely to emerge along with the other members of the metaphorical hierarchy. Wide use of prefabricated myth in the literature of

[1] Richard Volney Chase, *Quest for Myth* (Baton Rouge: Louisiana State University Press, 1949), pp. 105-31.

a given time indicates an integrated culture which feels strongly its indebtedness and relationship to the antecedent culture within which the myths originally emerged. The literature of Romanticism is particularly interesting for the variety and contradiction observable in its uses of myth: as packaged myth which nevertheless gained for a time a serious response (as in the case of Walter Scott's poems and novels), as radical reworkings of the conventional inheritance which failed to arouse much immediate interest (as in the case of Blake and Shelley), and as the bold and original mythologizing which was almost completely mysterious to many a literate mind of the day, to say nothing of popular effect (as in the case of what we regard as the most deeply original poetry of Wordsworth and Keats). The basic reason for this mythological cluttering of the historical scene was, of course, the inevitable disintegration of old orders and the naturally varied efforts of the poets to perform their mythologizing by pretending that the old constructions still breathed, by doing sometimes wonderfully neat work as morticians, or by daring to attempt the casting of new forms. But these historical matters are by way of parenthesis.

Two things more need to be added with reference to myth as the final member of the metaphorical hierarchy: (1) Whether viewed as the representation of an imaginative order with historical sanctions, or as the ever-recurrent creative effort to project an envisioned order standing in linked opposition to the mundane order, myth by its nature balances and overcomes the limitations of symbol and image. It lays out with persuasive completeness the ideal world toward which the symbol glances and it reaches back into the concrete world in which the image is rooted. (2) Myth, ultimately, may be indistinguishable from poetry except in those poems or parts of poems consisting of carefully regulated and mechanically patterned discursive statement self-consciously flavored with imagery.

To summarize: all serious literary thinking concerning the essential character of poetry recognizes metaphorical representation as poetry's distinctive function. This representation is invariably dualistic in formation and monistic in implicit intention. It seeks to incorporate data and ideas. Sign, image, symbol, and myth, respectively, are members of the metaphorical hierarchy in the name of which poems are made. The sign has no more than incidental interest or value as such, points exclusively to the dimension of abstract reason, and performs in poetry a low if necessary mechanical task. It betrays falsely metaphorical thought. The image possesses an interest of its own aside from its relation to the data of experience, for it resembles as closely as possible the appearances and sensory values of these data. The spirit of poetic imitation has begun to work here as it has not in the formulation of signs. The symbol has all the appearance of the image, but is of primary interest in its role as an incipient and suggestive guide toward a supermundane order. The myth, finally, performs the work of both image and symbol together and goes beyond them as it constructs with some elaboration the order suggested by symbol and at the same time makes use of a complex of images to retain its close kinship with experience at the sensuous level. It may be ultimately indistinguishable from poetry.

II

It is now time to consider the validity of these speculations with reference to actual poetic work. The choice of texts—Blake's "The Tiger," Coleridge's "The Rime of the Ancient Mariner," Keats' "Ode on a Grecian Urn," and Yeats' "Sailing to Byzantium" —naturally reflects a certain willfulness, but they are at least generally current. Further, their pertinence to the subject is easily recognized.

Certain surface characteristics of these poems offer obvious hints for comparative considerations of myth and symbol. All of the works, plainly enough, treat urgent matters involving the metaphysical dimension. They are symbolic poems in that they contain central images that achieve symbolic function as earlier defined. Accordingly, there is a minimum of discursive statement, and when it does occur it is found to be subdued by and in harmony with the symbolism of the poem as a whole. Traditional myths are to be found in all the poems, either prominently or peripherally. At the same time, none of these poems fails to exhibit original mythological achievement or a highly creative transmutation of traditional mythological materials. Blake and Coleridge maintain the power of Christian myth; Keats and Yeats find themselves, for whatever reasons, emancipated from any need for such a myth and attempt to use or create others. All four poets, however, are vehement and impassioned disciples of one or another significant mythological version of reality.

Blake's "The Tiger" is given body and coherence by tightly controlled focus upon a single image. This immediately assumes the character of symbol by the interest it engenders in the poet's vision on the other side of image, away from the mundane object of reference. While this symbol remains the organizing agent of the work throughout, as the poet explores the imagistic elements which give the symbol body, it makes myth by pointing to an order of creative activity and achievement imagined by the poet. This version of the myth of creation behind the tiger symbol possesses strong traditional features, yet it is at the same time an original construction having an intense vitality for the poet as he approaches it through the terrible concreteness of the tiger image. It is this savage and beautiful embodiment of cunning and ruthless brutality that moves the mind of Blake to envisage the origin of force, which in his passionately and paradoxically spiritual view is the origin of gentle passivity as well—as the lesser image of the lamb makes clear. He shows no interest in merely setting forth a prefabricated myth, though he has accepted, as suggested, some traditional elements because they remain vital for him and bear a true relation for him to the ultimate origin of his image.

"The Rime of the Ancient Mariner" is a deceptively simple structuring of enormous complexities and is thus, in the view of many, a triumph of poetic creativity. The myth or myths of which the poem makes the reader aware, which indeed enable the poem for the moment to stir him almost to faith, are made compelling by well-nigh every conceivable poetic device, as well as the nonpoetic one of discursive statement. Resisting the temptation to consider in any detail the character and function of these almost numberless elements in the poem, let us concentrate on the dominant and organizing presence, the character of the Mariner himself. This two-dimensional nature as symbolical or mythological is emphasized in a variety of ways, but at every point is to be understood as the incorporation of natural and supernatural characteristics. This identity is so extensively conveyed in terms of dramatic action, most of which occurs on the supernatural plane, that this poem may be called mythological rather than symbolic. Blake's tiger is never placed by the poet as a member of the mythological order suggested in that poem, though he is defined as a product of that order. Coleridge's Old Man of the Sea plays a far more complex role, since he is the chief performer in a pattern of progressive and withdrawing supernatural action; he is a vital member of the mythological order, absolutely controlled in his action and speech by that order, as even his natural appearance and his effect upon the Wedding Guest testify. This pattern of action represents a complete, rounded, profound embodiment of poetic vision. It is, in other words, a myth of high order exhibiting all features associated with myth whether regarded traditionally and historically or timelessly as the typical poetic gesture toward concretizing the ideal.

The richness of the mythological structure reared here may be accounted for, obviously, by reference to (as already suggested) myriad elements shaping the experience of the Mariner and operating, sometimes on the natural level, sometimes strictly on the supernatural, but all striving to link the two. This harmonizes such prominent details as the albatross, the ship, the figures of Death and Life-in-Death, the Wedding Guest and the ceremony, the water snakes, the sun, the moon, the blessed rain, and so forth. The chief artistic glory of the poem is the way in which the duality observed in the immediate human dilemma of the Wedding Guest (which has its appropriately frivolous and trivial side) on the one hand, and the Mariner's experience of spiritual rejection, isolation, and salvation on the other, is transformed into a unity. This is finally suggested in the change, described in subdued and childlike terms, that has come over the Wedding Guest—in the end "A sadder and a wiser man," his development corresponding on a trifling scale with that of the Ancient Mariner. The law of love has been revealed mythologically as valid for all dimensions.

Keats' "Ode on a Grecian Urn," perhaps his supreme effort, is most famous for the paradoxical assertion "Beauty is truth, truth beauty." This statement appears to defy poetry in two respects: (1) it is completely nonmetaphorical, and (2) it makes a claim for the aesthetic interpretation of experience apparently on the wrong grounds since, as was long ago suggested, the beautiful, or a certain species of it, is several removes from reality and hence surely cannot be equated with it. And the assertion is made the more offensive by the poet's immediately ensuing evaluation, "—that is all/Ye know on earth, and all ye need to know."

Like the Mariner's explicit statement to the Wedding Guest, the discursive remark "Beauty is truth, truth beauty" is dramatized by its assignment to a symbolic agent within the poem. This helps to remove at once the usual stigma of nontransfigured expression. But the really important thing about the remark is its use of the language of one dimension, that of earth (to use the image Keats employs in another way), to say something valid about another dimension, the mythological, and to suggest the vital relation between the two. Keats has consistently addressed the urn as indeed of the earth earthly: it is, he is careful to note at the beginning, the "foster-child of Silence and slow Time," and he is entirely aware toward the last that the lovely form is but a "cold pastoral." His address to the urn is in essence like that of Blake as the older poet questions his own very different image—it views the object as a timeless symbol which performs miracles of fusion in life. In Keats' handling the image becomes a symbol standing perfectly balanced between the mythological order and the mundane. With perfect aesthetic logic, the symbol acts as agent in such a way that we, with our rational limitations like those of the Wedding Guest, can understand and reduce to our usual terms the fusion that has taken place. The myth here is aesthetic, whereas those of Blake and Coleridge are religious. But there is no difference between the way in which they function in poetry or the value which they have within the poetic context.

One sees in Yeats' "Sailing to Byzantium" clear affiliations with the works just considered: the metaphysical theme posed in terms of contrasting imagery and method of statement; a central dynamic image transformed before our eyes; a voyage from earth to paradise and back; the affirmation that the two realms are integrally linked, antagonistic as they seem to be. Coleridge's Ancient Mariner is indeed "a tattered coat upon a stick" who sings "for every tatter in [his] mortal dress." Keats' urn is, in its way, "such a form as Grecian goldsmiths make" and is given words "to sing . . . Of what is past, or passing, or to come." The parallels are fascinating. Yet

Keats is closer because he uses the work of art as the symbolic agent
standing poised like a precious bulwark between, as Yeats puts it in
his other Byzantium poem, "that dolphin-torn, that gong-tormented
sea" or "all perplexities of mire and blood" (whichever phrasing,
as we see it, better fits our mortal state) and Byzantium: not, to be
sure, the City of God, but the aesthetic equivalent of it—the city
created by man in time and space out of his passion for a beauty
almost that of holiness. Blake's "The Tiger" is, relatively, in the
far background. Yet we must remember the fire and the furnace,
the images of divine creation's forge in that poem, as we encounter
Yeats' scandalous "holy fire," which he calls God's without really
meaning it, being only for the moment persuaded into faith. For
Yeats it is, as for Keats, the human impulse toward engagement in
art, not the eternally inscrutable God and His ways with beasts and
men, which is to be celebrated as meaningful, creative, and redeem-
ing. The myths of Blake and Coleridge are one thing, those of
Keats and Yeats another, however strikingly similar may be their
basic contrivances.

Yeats' poem, however, contains one element not so persistent and
closely woven in the other three poems, the tight and intimate
interplay of imagery with symbol and myth which is a characteristic
of this century's poetic idiom. To note the most prominent example
of this in the poem, one may observe how the imagery of music at
every crucial point accompanies the transformation of the key image
as it suffers the magic change effected by art from fleshly humanity
into the enduring object. There is music everywhere. Pan's pipes
blow lustily and reach crescendo in the first stanza. A higher music,
akin to Keats' "ditties of no tone" that strike only the spiritual ear,
furnishes in the second stanza the motive for the voyage to Byzantium, where, as we become aware in the third stanza, the ultimate
discipline is to be learned under the singing-masters of the soul—
the discipline that will purge away the last animal vestige. In the
fourth stanza the result of this discipline in music is found in the
created object, the bird fashioned "Of hammered gold and gold
enameling," singing now in its own right, not of "Whatever is
begotten, born, and dies," but of what is at once here and there,
in the limited dimension of time-space or in the transcendent abode
of the spirit's life. This provides a vivid and tautly patterned

ground of imagery, both constant and shifting, upon which the dramatic conversion action takes place as the old man—the symbol incorporating decaying flesh and vibrant spirit—achieves full mythical status as a member of a permanent order. Thus wondrously wrought is the harmony of image, symbol, and myth.

Suggested Readings

Cassirer, Ernst, *Language and Myth.* New York: Harper & Brothers, 1946.

Chase, Richard Volney, *Quest for Myth.* Baton Rouge: Louisiana State University, 1949.

Foss, Martin, *Symbol and Metaphor in Human Experience.* Princeton: Princeton University Press, 1949.

Prescott, Frederick Clarke, *Poetry and Myth.* New York: The Macmillan Company, 1927.

Tindall, William York, *The Literary Symbol.* New York: Columbia University Press, 1955.

Symbol and Myth in Modern
Rationalistic Societies

Gregor Sebba

Modern society is pervaded by the spirit of rationality; no area of social life has remained unaffected by technology, analysis, planning, control. Is there any room left for myth? Some see in myth merely a false belief. Myth, they say, thrives in the night of ignorance; it may linger on in the twilight of uncertainty, but the clear light of reason will kill it in the end. Others find that myth serves an important social function which guarantees its survival even in advanced societies:

> Every culture will create and value its own myths, not because it may not be able to distinguish between truth and falsity, but because their function is to maintain and preserve a culture against disruption and destruction. They serve to keep men going against defeat, frustration, disappointment; and they preserve institutions and institutional processes.[1]

A third view (see the article by Thomas J. J. Altizer, above) rejects the notion that myth is *false* belief and denies that modern rationalist society is capable of having myths in the true sense of the word. Myth, it holds, is an immediate awareness of a higher, truer, transcendent reality, a direct grasp of the Divine; modern man, incapable of such prerational awareness, is "doomed to live in an a-mythical world."

All three viewpoints stress the incompatibility of myth and rationalism. The second view is more realistic than the first: it recognizes that even false belief can have an essential social function. But is myth really nothing but *false* belief?

[1] R. Gotesky, "The Nature of Myth and Society," *The American Anthropologist,* LIV (1952), p. 530.

We might try to find a definition of myth that accommodates the various viewpoints and reconciles conflicting definitions of symbol and myth. However, it seems more useful to draw clear distinctions between related but different concepts and social situations to which the term "symbol" or "myth" has been attached. In the first part of this paper we will do so by developing a range of notions, rising from the simple concept of "mark" towards the complex notion of "myth." Then we shall try to assess the role which symbols and myths of a certain type play in modern rationalistic societies; a wide array of examples will suggest that they are considerably more frequent and important than one might expect.

FROM "MARK" TO "MYTH"

We draw two short lines on paper, thus:

$$+$$

We call this a *mark*. A mark is a mark, no more. It "means" nothing, it refers to nothing outside itself.

(1) We may, however, give this mark some arbitrary meaning. Let us think, for example, of a highway intersection. (This is what comes to mind if we see this mark in black on a yellow highway sign.) The relation between mark and intersection is obvious: the mark is an idealized image of the intersection; we shall call this an *isomorphic mapping*.[2]

(2) We now reconvert the isomorphic mapping into the original, meaningless, mark; and we place two other marks, one on each side of it:

$$a + b$$

In this new context our mark is at once recognized as a conventional sign that belongs to a "formalism" or "symbolism" and is often referred to as a "symbol." The sign (a "plus-sign") asks us to perform a certain operation on a and b, or, alternatively, tells us

[2] The concept of isomorphism as used in set theory and topology requires, beyond one-to-one correspondence, that the mapping should preserve certain structural characteristics of the original set. The application made below in the definition of *Symbol* satisfies this condition.

that a certain relationship exists between *a* and *b*. It is true that this sign may signify somewhat different operations and relationships, depending on the symbolism of which it forms a part; thus, plus-signs in a mathematical or physical equation signify something different from plus-signs in a chemical one. But in every case the meaning of the sign is, by convention, precise and unequivocal. Signs or "symbols" of this type (discussed by Leroy E. Loemker above) will not concern us further. The "symbols" we are interested in are of a different kind.

(3) We now reconvert our sign once more into a meaningless mark. Let us visualize this mark in the form of a small silver ornament attached to a fine chain and worn by a young lady we know. The mark now assumes yet another meaning; it becomes a "cross," and this cross we recognize as a "symbol"—but one very different from a plus-sign. It is no longer precise and unequivocal. It is merely suggestive. As a Christian symbol we distinguish it from, say, the Star of David, the Swastika, the Hammer-and-Sickle, the Crescent-and-Star. But these are broad distinctions. Undoubtedly the "cross" suggests widely different notions to different people; for instance, to a Protestant missionary, a Communist commissar, a college student dating the young lady. The best we can say is that this symbol —let us call it an *icon*—is a core of loosely clustered, widely diverging but overlapping associations.

(4) Let us now change the example. We consider a unit of fighting men at a time when armies are small and fight on foot. The men are to be trained for battle, and part of their training consists in developing conditioned reflexes to ensure instantaneous, "unthinking" obedience to commands. Some of these commands may be given by signs. For example, the order to rally may consist in raising a pole to indicate where the men are to gather. This action we call a *signal;* it communicates the message, and it triggers the conditioned reflex.

(5) It is easy to convert the signalling device into a device identifying the unit: the pole becomes a legion eagle, a pennant, a regimental flag, and so on. This identifies it, individualizes it, makes it enduring. It outlasts the men who at any given time form the unit; it takes part in their exploits, it acquires a "tradition," a "history." It thus becomes the *symbol* for the unit as distinct from the men

who form it. This symbol is not merely suggestive; it "stands for" the unit that endures—suprapersonal, historical, active. Let us now follow this symbol as it goes into action. The men are formed for battle, waiting. At the command, the symbol is inclined toward the enemy and moves forward at the head of the troops. This action is a signal, and it is more than that. The action is symbolic: the flag advances, but it does not fight. The action is isomorphic: the flag, the legion eagle, *does* what the fighting men are to do; and this makes its action powerful beyond the power of vocal commands or trumpet signals. For this is not just a piece of equipment being carried forward: as the flag moves to the attack, the symbol of the enduring unit with all its history, its tradition, advances toward the enemy. Carrying the flag towards battle and death is a *symbolic enactment*.

(6) In this enactment, the symbol acquires a *mythical quality*. Two episodes will help us understand this quality. When at a crucial turn in one of the battles of the Seven Years War the Prussian lines began to retreat under withering fire, Frederick the Great ordered his elite troops, the famous Grenadiers, to the charge. They stormed forward, but the attack began to falter. At this moment the King is said to have swung his cane at them, shouting: *"Kerls, wollt ihr denn ewig leben?"*—"Rascals, do you want to live forever?" Whether the anecdote is true or legendary hardly matters: it embodies an experience for which parallels can be found in the history of the best fighting units the world over.[3] But what is there in the grotesque invitation to die that would make unsophisticated soldiers court almost certain death? Another episode will help us find the answer.

Napoleon's army stands in the Egyptian desert, far from home, in unfamiliar country, facing an enemy different from any it has met. In this uncertain, unaccustomed, frightening situation, the General

---

[3] The sequel of the anecdote is no less typical. An old Grenadier is said to have called back to the King: "Look here, Fred [*Hör mal, Fritze*], I should think we did enough work today for our 13 cents pay!" The battle-proven veteran can afford this talk without being disgraced because his courage and instantaneous obedience to orders are unquestionable. An appeal to his honor will be heeded, regardless of the going rate of pay. Nevertheless, Frederick lost this battle (Kolin, June 18, 1757); it broke his record of invincibility.

addresses the army before the battle—July 21, 1798—with the famous words: "Think of it soldiers: from the summit of these pyramids forty centuries look down upon you!"

This order of the day takes the men out of the uncertain, threatening "here and now"; it places them squarely in the supraindividual context of history; it tells them plainly what they now must do. Frederick's question did the same: "Do you want to live forever?" Of course they do—normally. But not here, not now: the King's question tells them what they must do now. As history is enacted, the individual ceases to be an individual, a world unto himself. This is what Georges Sorel meant when he said that only in a mythical context can a soldier do what he must do, and yet feel that doing it makes sense; without this, he is a mere cog in a war machine, open to the intrusion of the self-preserving instinct, to the corroding influence of reasoning and doubt. Once he is within the mythical context, he is free to make his decisions with a feeling that everything is all right and settled, except for the one overriding question: Shall *we* win? This "we" is the impersonal, suprapersonal "we," the "cause," embedded in history. All meaning flows from it, and the small, timebound self knows it, if only for the brief moment of action—the moment that counts.

(7) While a mythical quality may inhere in objects, words, images, and so on, a *myth,* to follow the original sense of the word, is something narrower. A myth is a story, a narrative, a plot, an explanatory account; it may be historically true, legendary, or invented; but, for the believer, it is "truer than truth" and therefore highly impervious to refutation by a show of facts to the contrary. An example of a contemporary myth will show this.

After World War I, German nationalist students began to commemorate November 10 as "Langemarck Day," a day of solemn dedication to the fatherland. On that day in 1914 German regiments of war volunteers, mostly students fresh from the classroom, had attacked enemy positions near Langemarck, north of Ypres, taking them by storm despite frightful losses. The episode had no military significance, and anti-nationalist critics condemned the charge as a senseless waste of lives. What the students celebrated, however, was not the success of the action, but precisely these losses. It was claimed that these young men had recognized the hopelessness of the effort, yet went exultantly into death; as wave after wave broke down under murderous fire, some of them were said to have thrown away their useless rifles and to have stormed forward singing.

The "Myth of Langemarck," as the students themselves called it, is thus the story of an exemplary enactment; death at Langemarck was seen as blood sacrifice, pure and untainted by any thought of gain or success. The postwar students, uncertainly facing a world of collapsed ideals and irreparably broken hopes, seeing their fatherland beaten, dismembered, engulfed by "corroding alien ideologies," attacked by hostile forces from within and without, found in the Langemarck myth a beacon that gave assurance, direction, and meaning to their lives. The historicity of the story was not a matter of concern; whatever the "facts" might be, the event seemed rooted in the everlasting ground beneath the surface of history. In this sense the story was to them "truer than truth." This is what made it a myth.

Some Functions of Symbol

The "issues" at stake in elections are rarely defined or precisely definable; even in the case of a "yes" or "no" vote, taken to decide a seemingly precise question, the question is usually understood differently by different people; and those who understand it the same way are likely to differ in their interpretation of the consequences of the decision. How can a majority decision be reached when the electorate is split in so many ways that no majority can be formed? According to the classical theory of democratic processes, free and open discussion will produce a "will of the majority" by "clarifying" the issues and by persuading a majority or plurality of voters to agree on one course of action, one answer. Actually, suggestive symbols such as slogans, platform planks, personalities, symbolic signs, and so forth, play an essential role in this process. Since the symbol does not have a precise, unequivocal meaning, people of varying persuasions can accept it in the belief that they are all accepting the same thing for the same reason, when actually they are not.[4] Discussion will not help to reveal discrepancies of opinion either; if a number of people all agree that they are for "independence," it is not easy for them to find out that they are advocating dissimilar things. Who can say what people want when they vote for "independence," for "Dwight D. Eisenhower," for "The American Way of Life," for "Disarmament?" Any attempt to give precise meaning to the symbol would at once fragmentize the block of voters; the symbol enables the splinters to form a coalition capable of producing a decision.

The authoritarian case is illuminative. Those who fought to establish "Communism" in Russia had very different ideas about the meaning of "Communism," the consequences of adopting it, and the goals to pursue afterwards. Once victory had been won, a decision between these ideas and goals became inevitable; under the authoritarian principle, the decision in favor of one goal automatically made all dissenters heretics who either had to accept the "party line" or face a purge. But the "party line" is itself a suggestive symbol, though a narrower one than the symbol "Communism"; hence the need for further decisions which produce further splits and purges, a process which evidently has to go on until some mode of cooperation between main-liners and side-liners can be developed. The broader and the less defined the symbol (such as party line, platform) is, the easier it is to form and maintain a winning coalition.

Some iconic symbols attain a high degree of generality and serve as embodiments of the group, the body politic, as a whole; they become symbols of self-identification: flags, kings, anthems, emblems, and the rituals connected with them. These general symbols are necessarily vague in the extreme as far as their "meaning" is concerned; they are precise in a different sense: adherence to them defines who belongs to the body politic. Any discussion of their "meaning" either yields another equally vague stereotype, e.g. the explanation of the "meaning" of the American Flag as an affirmation of "The American Way of Life"; or else, if there are funda-

---

[4] The function of symbol and "stereotype" in democratic decision-making is worked out in Walter Lippmann's *Public Opinion* (New York: Harcourt, Brace & World, Inc., 1922), repeatedly reprinted in paperbound editions.

mental cleavages within the body politic, any search for a precise meaning of the symbol will bring these cleavages to the surface and produce open dissension. Thus the rejection of a national symbol by large segments of the body politic is a symptom of a fundamental lack of unity; and if these segments each have self-identification expressed in symbols of their own, then the question is justified whether one can speak of a body politic at all. The Weimar Republic of 1918 replaced the Black-White-Red of the Hohenzollern monarchy with the Black-Red-Gold of the democratic movement of 1848, but the new symbol was at once attacked and rejected by powerful segments in the nation; the flag struggle raged until a new symbol, the swastika flag of the Third Reich, became the new outward sign of unity and self-identification. The Austrian democratic republic of 1918 replaced the old symbols of the multi-national Habsburg empire by a set of new ones, to identify the new small residual state of "peasants, burghers, and workers"; though these new symbols were not attacked, they were not accepted either. People remained indifferent to them as they remained indifferent to the new state. On the other hand, the power of a generally accepted symbol was demonstrated in the years before the United States entered World War II, when the American Nazi Party had to recognize the Stars-and-Stripes as the national symbol, putting it in the place of honor when displaying its own swastika flag.

A living person may attain symbolic stature of great functional importance. The role of longevity among leaders is a case in point. The extraordinary feeling of stability in nineteenth-century Europe, despite rapid and radical changes, owes something to unusually long reigns like those of Queen Victoria of England and Francis Joseph of Austria, and to the long personal domination of Prince Bismarck in Prussia and Germany. After this stability collapsed in the First World War, other old men became symbols of order, from Stalin and Churchill to Adenauer, Eisenhower, and De Gaulle. The symbolic individual may become an icon, a living embodiment of order and hierarchical power, to the degree of acquiring mythical quality. The leader who grows to be a father image may, by his visible presence, strengthen stability—or at least impart a feeling of stability—in rapidly changing or dangerous times. The symbolization of an emerging order in a "Founding

Father" is particularly important in nascent societies. George Washington is one example; Kemal Mustapha Pasha, another "Founding Father," showed how well he understood his role when he adopted the name Atatürk or "Turk-Father."

Because of the power of the father image, the loss of the symbolic individual can have grave consequences, and succession is likely to raise difficult problems. The death of Francis Joseph of Austria, after a reign of no less than sixty-eight years, had profound symbolic implications, clearly seen by the Freud-disciple Paul Federn when he diagnosed the problem of the incipient Austrian republic of 1918 as that of a "Fatherless Society." [5] After the death of Stalin, the attack on the "cult of the personality," that is upon the symbolic role of the Stalin image, had to wait until the new leadership was firmly in the saddle; and though in Russia the demythologization was achieved without serious repercussions, the rule of orthodox party-line Communists in Hungary and Poland was shaken beyond repair, leading both countries to the brink of defection. Differing attitudes towards the Stalin symbol were, as usual, symptomatic. In Hungary, the Stalin monuments were toppled; in Czechoslovakia, Rumania, and the other hardcore satellites, these monuments remained standing, in obstinate if silent defiance of the demythologization ordered by Moscow; in Russia, the Stalin busts and pictures gradually disappeared, but demythologization had to stop short of depriving Stalin of his role of Founding Father, if the new leaders were to retain control. In Russia, the limits of demythologization could not have been marked more precisely: Stalin's body was to remain lying in state next to Lenin's for another half-decade, exempt from time, imperishable, sacrosanct. When the final step of reburial was taken it marked the end not of the Stalin myth (which is not dead even in Russia) but of the myth of monolithic Communist world unity. De-Stalinized Russia and Stalinist China brought the rift between them into the open.

A full treatment of the problem of social symbol and symbolization would have to go much deeper and extend much further than could be undertaken here. But even limited discussion suggests that the symbol problem should not be dismissed as irrelevant if not

[5] Paul Federn, *Zur Psychologie der Revolution: Die vaterlose Gesellschaft* (Leipzig-Wien: Anzengruber Verlag, 1919).

fictitious. Changing attitudes towards symbols old and new are almost always symptomatic and revealing, and the ability of leaders to attain symbolic status or to create powerful binding symbolisms is just as real a factor in the course of current events as are the more familiar, more calculable factors that enter into the analysis.

MYTH AND MYTHOPOEIA

Ideally, the citizen of an enlightened modern society uses the exercise of reason to guide him safely in the most troubled circumstances. Yet there are situations that make him feel powerless, bewildered, lost. He may be successful in his own endeavors, he may support all the right causes, yet evil threatens to engulf the society in which he lives, although reason, justice, might, and wealth are all on its side. The Greeks, under similar circumstances, sought refuge in myth:

Myth is a story which aims not at giving pleasure for its own sake but at alleviating perplexities which trouble prescientific man because his reason is not yet ready to grasp them. . . . The mythical explanation . . . is more emotional than rational and works not by describing cause and effect, but by associating one kind of experience with another and suggesting a connexion or similarity between them. . . . [Myths] bring the unknown into relation with the known and help to break down the barriers between men and the intractable mass of phenomena which surround them.[6]

What was true of "prescientific" Greek man whose reason could not yet grasp the perplexities of his time, is true of modern man who can no longer grasp them. However, even myths no longer furnish the essential explanations which man needs. After all, the habit of reasoning and calculating stands in their way. For modern man, daily life is one unending exercise in reasoning and acting upon reasoned analysis. Only where reasoning seems to be impotent, where "proper" action seems to be ineffective, do mythical beliefs comfortably fill the void, particularly when they appear superficially clothed in reasoned argument.

The myth-making power is not extinct. Mythopoeia occurs on various levels. Leaders who understand the power of myth and know

[6] Sir Maurice Bowra, *The Greek Experience* (New York: The New American Library, 1959), p. 115.

how to utilize it may deliberately create myth; mythical beliefs, mythical concepts, mythical stories may grow out of concrete social and political situations; finally there is the phenomenon of "grass-root mythopoeia," the spontaneous invention of stories capable of performing the function of myth, though they usually are short-lived and remain ineffective. An examination of two examples of grass-root myth-making will show the process at work.

An old lady in the deep South, plantation-born and plantation-raised, explained why Negroes have pale lips, palms, and soles. According to the story, God originally created all men black. But the better ones wanted to be pure and white like God; and God in His mercy created a pond in which anyone could dip and come out pure and white. And so all the young, strong, intelligent, God-loving people rushed to the pond and emerged white. The stupid, lazy, slow ones dawdled on the way; when they got to the pool, there was no water left, though the mud was still wet. They stomped around in this mud, tried it with their palms, and wiped the moisture on their lips. And this is why their lips, palms, and soles are pale, though their skin remained dark.

This story is a throwback to the "Why Story," a well-known type of story found among primitive people, in fairy tales, but also in documents of high importance, such as the story in Genesis that explains why the Snake crawls on his belly, and why there is enmity between him and man. The teller of the story about the Negroes admitted readily that this was "just a story" and not "really" true; but she also said that the story explained "why they are different from us" and why they are "not so smart." This difference, which, to her, was a matter of daily observation and lifelong experience, became intelligible by being linked with her religious beliefs and was corroborated by the reference to physical characteristics of the colored people. The story thus strengthened her beliefs in the face of scepticism: the story was "truer than truth."

Our second example is taken from a conversation between two poorly dressed elderly women, overheard in the mid-1930's in a cheap Vienna coffee house. The first woman announced that there would be another world war in five years, and that it would completely destroy Austria "and all the countries." Her companion was sceptical and asked her how she knew. The answer (which was apparently

convincing) was as follows: Ninety-five years ago, the great Emperor
Napoleon had called the leaders of the Jews of the world to a
secret meeting at Schloss Schönbrunn in Vienna. At that meeting,
the Jews laid out the history of the next hundred years and wrote
it down in a secret book. They planned for one great war in 1914;
at the end of these hundred years, there was to be the greatest war
yet. After that war, they would meet again and lay out the history
of the next hundred years.

The story refers to historical events, though they are hopelessly
garbled. Napoleon did stay at Schönbrunn, though not in the 1830's
(he died in 1821); he entered Schönbrunn for the first time in 1805.
Napoleon did convoke the so-called Paris Sanhedrin, an assembly
of rabbis of France (not of Jewish leaders throughout the world)
and charged it with working out legal principles for the government of Jews in France. The Sanhedrin never met in Schönbrunn,
of course. The two historical facts, Napoleon's stay at Schönbrunn
and the convoking of the Sanhedrin, are linked in the woman's
account with the "Protocols of the Elders of Zion," which were
popularly believed to be genuine. The result is an "historical
account" which "explains" the First World War, the collapse of
Imperial Austria in 1918, the Great Depression, the bloody civil
uprisings in Austria of 1927 and 1934, catastrophes which the
women had witnessed but could not possibly understand in terms of
cause and effect. The story "explains" the past, the present, and
the future by a simple mechanism (a world conspiracy by powerful,
immensely wealthy leaders). The dimly remembered genuinely
historical elements give it credibility.

Stories like these are mere bubbles, and of no significance in themselves. However, they exemplify the way in which myth helps
people "understand" social and political reality that is at once
mysterious and threatening. Another, equally important, function
of myth consists in producing and maintaining homogeneity of
feeling and solidarity within the body politic. These two functions
are closely interrelated, though analytically separable. We shall
survey general significant types of social myth, beginning with
examples of explanatory myths and moving towards myths of
solidarity.

1. *The Devil. The Great Conspiracy. The Purge. The Scapegoat.*
One's own nation is good, benevolent, powerful, rich. Why is its
supremacy threatened? One's own way of life is superior. Why do
others reject it? One's own nation has been defeated; now it is
weak and helpless. Why can it not rise again?

When a nation is strong, successful, and supremely confident, it
need not ascribe mysterious power and sinister purposes to its
enemies. It can think of the enemy in purely rational terms; no
recourse to myth is needed, and attempts to construe such a myth
are likely to fail. The Germany of Bismarck and William II was
in this position. When William II conjured up the demon of
"Yellow Peril" (*Die gelbe Gefahr*), the specter of a tidal wave of
the yellow races rising against white world domination, the idea
fell flat. But when the Reich of William II collapsed, against all
expectation and despite great victories in the field, when the weak
Weimar Republic was struggling to maintain itself at home and to
regain European and world status by adapting itself to new, unfamiliar conditions in the postwar world, mythological explanations
were sought and found to explain the past catastrophe and the
unfamiliar present, and to rally people for a supreme new effort.
In such situations, the enemy is no longer seen rationally, the way
a business man sees a competitor. Instead, an old archetype arises
in varying forms: the archetype of the devil.

During the disastrous German inflation after World War I, when
cities and towns printed their own "emergency money" (*Notgeld*),
one city printed such money on silk, as a collector's item. The
artistic design included symbolic representations of the powers
causing the inflation: the International Jew, the Wall Street
Capitalist clutching his money bag, Usury wildly cheered by un-
savory speculator types. The faces of all these symbolic figures were
familiar: they all looked like the Devil.

Today, the United States and Soviet Russia are entangled in a
cold war, against the ghastly background of nuclear destruction.
Worldwide intelligence networks operate now subtly, now massively,
organizing espionage, infiltrating saboteurs, instigating and feeding
revolts and invasions. The two most powerful, vigorous, activist
nations in the world are both stymied everywhere, just when everything seemed to go their way. Why?

The Russian sees his country victorious and invincible, its political and economic system irresistible: the whole world is longing for its blessings. Capitalism was supposed to crumble long ago. Yet the irresistible World Revolution is desperately, unaccountably slow. What is holding it up? The Devil. The Imperialist Warmongers are plotting and scheming everywhere; Wall Street Capitalism is financing them. No wonder the peaceful, altruistic Russians are blocked.

The American sees his country victorious and invincible, its political and economic system superior: the whole world is longing for the American standard of living and the American way of life. Yet the West is on the defensive. No sooner is one situation brought under control, then several other "emergencies" arise, equally threatening and intractable. Why? Because of the Devil. World Communism is at work everywhere, secretly supported and paid by Moscow. No wonder the peaceful, altruistic American nation is blocked.

In the Arab world, the just aspirations of the Arab peoples are frustrated. Why? Because of the Devil. The Jew controls everything.

When the Weimar Republic fell and Hitler took power, all problems became exceedingly simple for the Germans. The guileless German had been exploited, weakened, enslaved, kept down by the Devil. Once the purity of the race was restored, once the Devil was destroyed, everything would be right again.

The underlying facts are one thing, the mythical archetype is another. Only under conditions of fundamental insecurity and inability to understand events do known facts such as the existence of a worldwide intelligence and propaganda network give rise to archetypal explanations. Where no need for such radical simplification exists, the facts themselves do not produce the mythical Devil image. For example, the classical model of worldwide intelligence operations, the British Intelligence Service, never produced the image of a British World Conspiracy.

In the modern world, the Devil has all the characteristics of the medieval Devil, translated into modern terms. The Devil is ubiquitous, insidious, powerful, and morally corrosive. He must be identifiable and recognizable as an image, but unidentifiable and disguised when at work. Groups that can serve as Devil images must therefore be ubiquitous, insidious, powerful, morally corrosive; they must be identifiable as groups, but capable of disguise—indeed, of making themselves invisible—in their operations. "The Russian people" or "The American people" can therefore not serve as Devil. They are geographically localized, and they are much like other people, once you come to know them. But Communism, Wall Street Capitalism, Imperialism, Freemasonry, and so on, meet the requirements.

The operations of the fiend are worldwide and secret. There exists a World Conspiracy aiming at nothing less than the utter destruction of its foes, followed by world domination. The Communist World Conspiracy works through espionage, sabotage, and revolution, the Capitalist Conspiracy through incitement to war and through "spies, wreckers, and saboteurs." The Jewish Conspiracy according to Hitler works through race-mixing, cultural poisoning, and warmongering against the German *Volk*.

The Great Conspiracy has a secret Master Plan which may accidentally become known. After Pearl Harbor the so-called "Tanaka Memorial" was used to prove the existence of a secret Japanese master plan. This memorandum, presumably written in 1927 by the Japanese statesman Baron Gi-Ichi Tanaka, "outlines a planned imperialist conquest of China, the Pacific, and finally the world," to quote the 1960 edition of Colliers' Encyclopedia. The most famous Master Plan known is the *Protocols of the Elders of Zion*.

This document is faked; even those who use it know that it is faked, but this does not diminish its credibility for them. When Hermann Rauschning reminded Hitler of the fact that the *Protocols* he was citing were a patent forgery, Hitler angrily retorted that this was irrelevant. Their "inner truth" was the more evident for their being faked. As soon as he had read them, he added, he had realized that his own master plan would have to be designed after this pattern—"in our own way, of course." It did not matter whether the *Protocols* were genuine; what mattered was that they were "true." [7]

[7] Hermann Rauschning, *Gespräche mit Hitler* (New York: Europa Verlag, 1940), p. 224-225. Rauschning reports a conversation with Hitler, before 1936, in which the Führer rejected the idea of wiping out the Jews on the grounds that the Jew would have to be invented if he did not exist: ". . . you need a visible, not an invisible enemy" (p. 223). In fact, he invented Jews whenever he needed them, e.g., "the Jew Rosenfeld" (i.e., Franklin Delano Roosevelt).

The Great Conspiracy works through spies, saboteurs and wreckers; it subverts the faithful and gains adherents among the very ranks of the enemy. One can no longer trust anybody: there is treason in high places. Vigilance alone is not enough. From time to time the poison must be symbolically eliminated from the body politic. This is the purpose of *the Purge.*

The Purge uncovers and eliminates the traitors; it sets a warning example to the wavering; above all, it morally cleanses the body politic. To do this, the Purge must be more than punishment for crime committed. It must cast out those who are tainted. This is not a matter of individual guilt. The guilty are *punished,* but the innocent are *sacrificed.* Suspicion is enough to mark them out. The Great Conspiracy has an irrational dimension; to be effective, the Purge must have this same dimension. The very incongruity between the grounds for indictment and the severity of the treatment guarantees its efficacy. Underlying the Purge is the Blood Myth which calls for Redemption through the Sacrifice of the Innocent.[8]

When the Purge runs up against a Symbol, a critical situation may arise. When Senator McCarthy moved against a dentist who was a major in the Army, he met no obstacles, for a dentist is no symbol, even if he is an Army major. But when the Senator put General Zwicker on the stand, he attacked a symbol. The implications went far beyond the matter of Army morale. The attack on one general was an indirect attack upon the other general, the father image in the White House, the preserver of order. The fall of the Senator initiated the years of the Eisenhower calm: the nation accepted the great symbol as powerful and capable of acting decisively whenever it chose to do so. Whether it did act or not ceased to be a matter of concern.

2. *The Divine Origin. The Mission.* If a nation feels its moral foundations or its independence threatened, if it is in search of a

---

[8] See Robert A. Horn, *Groups and the Constitution* (Stanford: Stanford University Press, 1956), pp. 177-78 on the legal drive against subversion in the United States as "a great symbolic rite rather than as a practical policy" and as a pledge to defend threatened values. Horn sees the dangers of the "ritual" as a substitute for effective antisubversive action, as distracting from dangers abroad, and as a threat to innocent persons; however, "it is not dangerous simply because it is a ritual"; moreover, it mobilizes emotions needed to sustain a very hard national effort.

justification of its goals and policies, it may seek recourse in a myth that idealizes its origins, gives its endeavors moral sanction, or endows it with a superior "mission." The Germans found elements of their myth of origin in the *Germania* of Tacitus which described their ancestors as good-humored, almost childlike innocents of superior morals and incomparable courage in war; they found them in the Nibelungen saga, an epic of a group of noble fighters welded together by loyalty unto death, courageously accepting their destiny, going with open eyes to their doom, and perishing through treachery and brutality, a lost island of the brave in a raging sea of enemies. The Nibelungen saga also gave them the Siegfried-Hagen myth of the sun hero who, invulnerable except for the one unprotected spot on his shoulder, is treacherously killed from behind by the sinister foe.[9] All this went into the Nordic Myth of the pure master race, a race naturally endowed with all the qualities of leadership and creativity but engulfed by a hostile world of evil subhumans against whom Nordic man would not prevail until he decided to extirpate the Devil (kill the Jews, abolish Wall Street Capitalism, destroy Red Communism, shake off corrupting liberal-democratic ideologies) and take his destiny in his own pure and mighty hands. The outline of this myth is well enough known. What is not equally well known is the enormous effort that was made to rewrite world history, from its very beginnings, in the light of this myth of origin, an effort that was by no means confined to the propaganda of the Nazi Party; in fact, this "reconstruction" of history preceded the rise of Hitlerism by many decades and helped pave the way for it.

The American myth of origin is very much simpler and quite unassuming. It finds its expression in one short sentence that describes the forebears of the present-day Americans as "those sturdy pioneers who carved a nation out of a wilderness." This sentence seems, on the surface, to be no more than mild Fourth-of-July oratory. Its mythical character is revealed when one considers that these few words manage to eliminate from the origins of the nation the two groups that bother the national conscience: the immigrants

[9] This myth itself is a piece of secularized Nordic mythology: the slaying of the youthful God Baldur, victim to the scheming of the wicked god Loki who had discovered the only weapon that could hurt Baldur.

and the Indians. The "sturdy pioneers" are "early Americans," and the "wilderness" from which the nation is carved is a natural wilderness that belongs to nobody. In forgetting the immigrants, the myth affirms the homogeneity of the nation, and in forgetting the Indians it affirms the morality of taking their land.

The idealization of national origin derives from the more ancient notion of a divine origin, of the "chosen people." It places the origin of the nation in a numinous light. Something unique, heroic, blessed has happened, something pure and strong; whatever the present dangers may be, the origin is secure.

"Missions" are much less fundamental, though a belief in them can be a powerful factor in shielding a nation against dissension in regard to foreign policy. The least fundamental "missions" are those that are obvious rationalizations of existing policies: the "white man's burden," or Imperial Austria's mission of "carrying culture eastward." Such rationalizations are open to destructive ridicule, as when an Austrian writer commented that Austria had carried so much culture eastward that there was hardly any left at home.[10] However, the myth of the historical mission may be quite strong when linked with the myth of the good engaged in a death struggle against the evil: to "make the world safe for democracy," to save the world from Communism, to destroy the imperialist warmongers.

3. *The Historical Myth.* The purpose of historical myth consists in making historical events compatible with a nation's view of itself. Since a full understanding of history is impossible, since all historiography must be selective, an historical image acceptable to the common man must be drawn with a few simple strokes, as the following allegations show.

The Russian knows that Japan, undefeated after nearly four years of ineffective American attack, succumbed in a matter of days when the might of the Soviet power struck. He knows that Russia defeated Hitler by her own strength, despite the wicked refusal of her allies to open a second front until Russia had been bled white. The Westerner knows that Russia did not declare war upon Japan until

[10] Daniel Spitzer in his *Wiener Spaziergänge* of May 27, 1888. See Spitzer, *Wiener Abstecher,* ed. W. A. Bauer (Vienna: Wiener Drucke, 1923), p. 88.

Japan was crushed and just about ready to surrender. He knows that the Normandy invasion saved Russia, just as Lend-Lease had prevented Russia from collapsing. The German nationalists knew that in 1914-18 Germany had remained "unconquered in the field" (*im Felde unbesiegt*) and that she had lost the war through a "Stab in the Back" (*Dolchstoss*) administered by socialist, communist, pacifist traitors incited, supported, and paid by her enemies. Hagen had once more killed Siegfried. The man who had led the undefeated German army in orderly fashion from its battle positions deep in France back to the Reich, Field Marshal von Hindenburg, rose to symbolic stature, a stature denied to General Ludendorff, the brain behind him. It is of the highest significance that no such myth has so far developed in Germany since the Second World War.

It would be wrong to look at historical myth as a convenient lie, designed to bolster a people's self-righteousness. One's understanding of history must be reasonably consistent with the facts one knows about it. That these facts are but part of the very large picture which one does *not* know, is not easily recognized or admitted. And even if admitted, it is impossible to turn this admission into something useful: the whole, the picture, remains outside one's experience, and the few specific traits one *concretely* knows are the only ones that can affect one's vision of history. Hence, historical myth thrives on the common man's inability to see—much less to analyze, least of all to understand—the whole of historical development; historical myth satisfies his desire to achieve a view of history in which the "unchallengeable facts" as he sees them are not challenged by other, irreconcilable, facts. One example will suffice to show the mechanism at work.

To the American of the 1920's and 1930's the inferiority of a Communist economy was more than an article of faith. Every known fact proved it; the Communists themselves could not deny it. They merely called the inefficiency of the Russian economy a phenomenon of infancy, soon to be outgrown. Thus, several beliefs came to be accepted rather generally in the West: (1) A Communist economy will never be able to match the achievements of a comparable capitalistic economy. (2) A Communist economy is a poor economy: it cannot make a superior financial effort. (3) Industrial skills and "know-how" cannot develop in an economy without competition and profit motive. (4) Science thrives only where freedom reigns.

Consequently, Russia was held incapable of producing an atom bomb after World War II in less than ten years, if at all. She could not afford the financial burden; her science was obsolete; even given the blueprints and the money, she would lack the industrial know-how. When Russia unexpectedly produced the bomb only a few years after the end of the war, Westerners had to face the choice between changing their basic beliefs about the Russian economy, or seeking an explanation consistent with these beliefs. Following the revelation of Russian nuclear espionage in Great Britain and the United States, the second course was taken: Russia had stolen the secret. This explanation was consistent with the belief in the inferiority of Russian science and Russian industry. Russia's unexpected space achievements made this belief untenable. With the successful launching into orbit of the first Russian satellite, a whole array of new facts, hitherto neglected or argued away, forced its way into plain view. The result is a far more realistic appraisal of Russia's capabilities as an aggressive, expansionist power, and a slowly growing understanding of the magnitude of effort it takes to check and contain this power.

Historical myth, then, is an incomplete historical rationalization which resists rational criticism because it is emotionally satisfactory and because the few historical facts it uses are accepted as a guarantee of its historical truth. Under favorable circumstances, a clash between historical myth and historical fact will lead to the gradual disappearance of myth in favor of more rational views, as the example above shows. However, if the new facts are emotionally unacceptable, historical myth may deepen, divorce itself further from reality, and seek its roots in a suprapersonal, fully mythical experience and world view.

4. *The Blood Myth.* When in November 1918 the defense of Germany's Western Front became hopeless, the High Command advised Emperor William II to abdicate in order to make possible an armistice, an orderly withdrawal, and a negotiated peace. But where was the Emperor to go? The older generals, headed by Field Marshal von Hindenburg, advised him to go into exile; some younger leaders wanted the Emperor to die on the battlefield in a

last charge against the enemy, leading a small band of voluntary followers sworn not to return alive.

The argument was that the Emperor's death in battle would give the monarchy such mythical strength that its eventual restoration would be inevitable. The proposal was opposed as impractical; modern war no longer leaves room for chivalry, and there was no guarantee that the Emperor would die; he might be wounded, perhaps even taken prisoner, with incalculable consequences. The Emperor himself left the decision to the High Command, which adopted the safe rational course of action.

The younger generals may have been vindicated by the outcome. With the flight of the Emperor to neutral Holland, the idea of the monarchy died. But the question of the proper action in November 1918 kept alive. In 1924 a Munich paleontologist, Edgar Dacqué, published a famous book in which he claimed that man, in paleontological times, has passed through a stage of immediate magic powers over nature which he lost to the degree as Reason gave him technological power. However, the old powers still archaically reach into rationalist society; for example, the Blood Sacrifice can change the course of history: the Blood Sacrifice of Christ is still celebrated daily in mystical communion. In this context Dacqué contended that the Blood Sacrifice of the German leaders in November 1918 would have unleashed untamable daemonic powers. A new Sun Myth would have arisen to make the German nation capable of a Revolution very different from the "dirty" one that actually took place in 1918: "But of this transcendence of facts and life we have no knowledge any more; even our princes and leaders have become technicians and scientists." [11]

In the Blood Myth, the supraindividual realm of myth manifests itself at its deepest. At the outset of World War II it was predicted that Hitler, if he lost the war, would commit suicide, preferably in such manner that there would be no body left behind—wholly disappearing from earth, as it were. This was the only fitting end of this Wagnerian *Götterdämmerung* in which calculation and myth were inextricably intermixed. What has so far prevented his blood sacrifice from becoming efficacious is the fact that Germany

[11] Edgar Dacqué, *Urwelt, Sage und Menschheit* (4. erg. Auflage, München-Berlin: Oldenbourg, 1927), p. 328-29.

has lost its key position on the European and global chessboard, and that the people of West Germany have found their new small position quite comfortable and reasonably secure. During the 1920's and 1930's their position was different, and these were the years when the Blood Myth flourished and was deliberately fostered and utilized, especially in Germany and Italy. We have already noted the Myth of Langemarck; there were other attempts to create Blood Myths, all on the part of the ultranationalists of various color and conviction, in contrast with the fundamentally rationalistic attitude of their center and left-wing foes. At the core of these Blood Myths were the Martyrs. Their death was not merely a memorable and an exemplary event; it was the source of new strength. This theme was elaborated and presented in impressive symbolizations, presented with the aid of the most refined methods of modern advertising and mass psychology.

At the Fascist Memorial Exhibition in Rome (1933-34) a huge, black, circular, vaulted hall was dedicated to the "Martyrs of Fascism." In the center of the dark room rose a gigantic white cross, seemingly floating on glowing red light issuing from around its base, the only light in the room. White bands of writing circled the vault, row upon row, one word interminably repeated:

PRESENTE! PRESENTE! PRESENTE! PRESENTE! PRESENTE! PRESENTE! The martyrs were answering the Fascist ritual of the Roll Call of the Dead: "Present!" "Present!" "Present!" . . . Beneath the vault, on the black walls, were the combat pennants of the Fascist storm troopers' units, each inscribed with the name of a martyr; for whenever one "died for Fascism," a new troop was founded in his name, springing from his blood, as it were.[12]

In Nazi Germany, Horst Wessel, an adolescent killed in a political brawl, was made official martyr, and the Horst Wessel song became the anthem of Hitlerism: "Comrades whom Red-Murder . . . shot to death are marching with us in spirit." The brutality and inhumanity which Hitler inculcated in his followers from the beginning, when power was very far off indeed, had profound mythological as well as psychological roots and effects. Nazism was

[12] Partito Nazionale Fascista, *Mostra della rivoluzione fascista* (Roma, 1933-XI), pp. 50, 227-229.

designed as a blood movement; shedding blood cemented the movement; cruelty and vicious contempt for the life of others made it a brotherhood outside the reach of humane considerations and calculating reason. The war seems to have killed this blood mythology; it proved the superiority of rational organization, analysis, and decision.

Although Communism is thoroughly rational in its origins and opposed to Fascist mythology, the body of Lenin lies, preserved, in state; to a generation born after the struggle for power and survival, it represents the numinous origin of the Soviet power in the visible form of flesh surviving corruption and decay. This symbolization is the style of the 1920's; even in the rationalistic democratic societies, shrines of the Unknown Soldier then rose in memory of the great blood sacrifice. No such symbolization occurred after the Second World War: the great blood sacrifice of 1914-18 had proved inefficacious, and from the blood of the heroes of the First World War had sprung nothing but disorder, insecurity, and new bloodshed.

The more rationalistic a society, the more resistant it is to the Blood Myth. In the United States this myth is as good as absent, though a faint trace of it surrounds the figure of Abraham Lincoln. Of the three great monuments in Washington, the Jefferson Memorial is what its name says—a memorial; the Washington Monument is what its name says—a monument (which, in its cold rationality, falls short of being a symbol); but the Lincoln Memorial, with the huge, brooding, superhuman figure sitting there as if enthroned, has a distinct mythical quality.

5. *Myth and State.* The mainstream of political science in the nineteenth and the early twentieth century was strictly rationalistic. Theory of government, if it was not a rationalization of ethical feelings, was a kind of engineering science which studied the workings of political institutions. The problem of symbolization was consequently ignored. Institutions that had no evident practical usefulness and violated the ethical principles of government came under theoretical attack.

The problem of political symbolization and the mythical roots of the state came into the open after the First World War, when old

constitutions tumbled and new, modern democratic-republican constitutions had to be written. Here was the great opportunity for
first-rate constitutional engineering, and some of the new constitutions were indeed masterpieces of rational construction, as functional as an air-conditioned assembly-line plant. They incorporated
the best thinking of the experts, as well as the experience of states-
men who fully understood the theory as well as the practice of
government. Outstanding from the technical viewpoint were the
Austrian Constitution of 1920 and Germany's Weimar Constitution. But the work of the professors did not stand up under hard use.

The Austrian Constitution underwent change after change, until,
in 1933, it became inoperative. The Weimar Constitution fell the
same year, having patently failed to provide stable government. The
much older Constitution of the French Third Republic did outlast
the Second World War, but collapsed when its built-in inability to
produce stable government brought the country to the brink of
catastrophe over the Algerian crisis.

The failure of some of the new, rationally and ethically outstanding constitutions became patent at once. As a result, the premises
upon which they rested came under sharp scrutiny during the
1920's and 1930's, and the problem of symbolization and myth
came to the fore. Totalitarianism opposed to constitutional rationalism a form of government based on a carefully developed myth
of the state, rejecting not only the instruments created by Western
political tradition, but casting the ethical ideals of that tradition—
equality, justice, freedom—into the role of the Devil. In Russia,
the Marxian conception of the Dictatorship of the Proletariat became the mythological foundation of the monolithic Party State.

The most interesting and rewarding theoretical work, however,
resulted from a shift in viewpoint from the technical characteristics
of a system of government to the underlying socio-political structure
needed to give it stability and endurance. These studies led to a
new understanding of homogeneity in the body politic, based chiefly
on an analysis of those nations whose system of government had
proved most stable and efficient: Great Britain, the United States,
Switzerland, and the Scandinavian countries. It appeared that this
stability was not simply attributable to the "excellence of the institutions of the country," as the eighteenth-century formula had it, nor

to the Wisdom of its Founding Fathers, nor to the superiority of the democratic idea, but to a certain type of homogeneity in the body politic and to adequate symbolization of the established political order. This homogeneity, it was suggested, was rooted in a suprarational, decidedly mythical, feeling of "togetherness" which prevented the body politic from breaking up into irreconcilably hostile factions. This made the constitutions of these countries workable even under severe stress. From this viewpoint, the most rationalistic modern states appeared to be *mythically* superior to some antirationalistic totalitarian states that had to impose a myth of the state from above precisely because no political myth held the body politic together.[13]

MYTH AS HISTORICAL FORCE

Rational analysis can determine the best means for attaining a given end; therein lies its strength. It cannot decide which ends to adopt; therein lie its weakness and its limitations. To decide between conflicting ends, reason must use some criterion, some scale of values, by which to judge these ends. But this criterion, these value-scales, must again be selected out of a number of differing, conflicting values. This in turn requires a still higher criterion to be selected by means of a yet more elevated one, and so forth until in the end one criterion, one scale of values is adopted *axiomatically,* that is, without weighing "advantages" and "disadvantages," in other words, without calculation.

For example, the best means of attaining equality under existing conditions can be rationally ascertained. But why strive for equality rather than for inequality? This question can be rationally dealt with if we have a principle by which we may assess the advantages and the disadvantages of either, such as the principle of justice, or the principle of social stability. In the end, either the process of rational decision turns into an infinite regress, or else it ends where some principle presents itself with overwhelming force. In practice, the principles under which rational decision operates are applied as

[13] Many outstanding antidemocratic theorists looked with envy upon Great Britain as a model of political organization for viability. So did Oswald Spengler, the prophet of impending Caesarism.

a matter of fact; it would not occur to the decision-maker to question them. In other words, they are axiomatic.

It follows that rationalistic methods of bringing about change will work where generally accepted goals exist, or where a decision between conflicting goals can be made within the framework of accepted principles of greater generality. The process of change within a framework of accepted principles is called *reform*. Changes that cannot be brought about by reform may be brought about by *revolution*. We define revolution as a process of change which involves the creation of a new axiomatic system of governing principles or values. This implies that the revolutionary change from one axiomatic system to another is grounded in nonrational decision. And since such decision arises from profound, basic, prerational belief, revolution is mythical in origin. Even the rationalist revolution began with the ascendancy of the Myth of Reason.

A consideration of the position of a leader in a crucial decision-situation leads to similar conclusions. In the normal, nonrevolutionary course of events, the leader makes his decision as a technician and craftsman, with full command over available information. But how does he make decisions in situations of utmost uncertainty where rational calculation cannot produce a clear argument in favor of one course? The extreme case is one in which the uncertainty of the outcome casts its shadow over the principles used in judging such outcomes. In this situation, reasoning may paralyze the decision-maker as it would paralyze a soldier in action who suddenly begins to wonder why he is fighting and why he should go on fighting. The eventual decision (or failure) to act may be the product of personal characteristics, of habit, of an inclination to gamble blindly, of outside forces, or of chance; in all these cases it is fortuitous, not rational. If, however, the decision is made out of deep, ultrarational commitment to an ultimate goal or value, its roots are in the mythical realm.

Situations of this kind are quite common where leaders of an established rational order confront revolutionary forces. If the habit of rational decision is deeply ingrained, it may undermine the will to act and the courage to act. The classical case is the failure of the mighty Social-Democratic Labor Party in Prussia to stop the revolutionary impetus of National Socialism and its conservative helpers.

The party had at its command the resources of the Prussian government, the Berlin Police, trained and equipped for civil war, and a vast organization of its own party members, which was also armed and equipped for civil war. However, the will to use these forces in earnest was lacking, chiefly because the leaders, thoroughly trained and steeped in Marxist rationalistic casuistry, had become incapable of acting out of sheer commitment. They made decisions by weighing the issues, calculating the possible consequences, debating, arguing, and finally voting. Whenever the rank-and-file was on the brink of going into action, the leaders held them back with the assurance that "ballots, not bullets" would bring them victory. Chancellor Franz von Papen, a conservative in league with Hitler, recognized this weakness and acted on it. On July 20, 1932 he sent one lieutenant and two enlisted men to the Prussian Minister of the Interior Franz Severing to depose him. The leader, instead of having the three men ushered out or arrested, declared: "I yield to force," locked his desk, and went home. He had made the reasonable decision not to test the strength of the force to which he yielded. The Myth of Reason being dead, the door was soon open for the Blood Myth to enter unobstructed.[14]

CONCLUDING REMARKS

As one brings symbol and myth into focus, the rational character of modern societies recedes into the background. To restore the full picture it would now be necessary to analyze the rational forces which are at work in such societies, and to show the connections and the relationships between them and the nonrational forces. One need only consider the power and all-pervading

[14] See Serge Chakotin [recte Chakhotin], *The Rape of the Masses: The Psychology of Totalitarian Propaganda* (London: Routledge & Kegan Paul Ltd., 1940), ch. 7. Chakhotin was a propaganda engineer who believed that "psychologically correct" campaigns could win the battle of symbols for Hitler's Socialist foes. His failure to convince the mythless Socialist leaders is as instructive as is his naïve faith in political advertising as a myth substitute and myth generator.

influence of technology to recognize the limits it sets to action that stems from mythical commitment. Technology, to say nothing of other rational forces, lays down conditions which no modern society can evade. This means that the problems of myth and symbol arise under conditions imposed by the spirit of rationality. Moreover, under the rule of this spirit, myth and symbol themselves become tools of rational socio-political engineering. Finally, modern man's capability to experience myth, to act out of mythical commitment, to understand symbolizations, is severely limited; in nontotalitarian societies, this capability is constantly under weakening attack by "unauthentic" modes of life, without counteraction from above.

Nonetheless there are realms where myth and symbol still hold their place, not as survivors of antediluvian or primitive states in man's development, but as essential, autonomous functions of the body politic, be it healthy or diseased. An examination of these functions is necessary to the understanding of modern societies; it brings into view a factor that plays its part in old-established as well as in nascent states and societies; and it raises important questions which cannot yet be answered in a satisfactory way.

List of Editors and Authors

(*All, of Emory University*)

THOMAS J. J. ALTIZER, Associate Professor of Bible and Religion. Ph.D., University of Chicago, 1955. A comparative theologian, Dr. Altizer is the author of *Oriental Mysticism and Biblical Eschatology*.

WILLIAM A. BEARDSLEE, Professor of Bible and Religion, Director of the Institute, 1957-1961. Ph.D., University of Chicago, 1951. A Biblical scholar, Dr. Beardslee is the author of *Human Achievement and Divine Vocation in the Message of Paul*, and is currently studying the relation between New Testament faith and culture.

J. HARVEY YOUNG, Chairman of the Department of History and Professor of History. Ph.D., University of Illinois, 1941. Dr. Young, whose field is American social and intellectual history, is the author of *The Toadstool Millionaires, A Social History of Patent Medicines in America before Federal Regulation*.

RICHARD HOCKING, Chairman of the Department of Philosophy and Professor of Philosophy. Ph.D., Yale University, 1935. Dr. Hocking recently collaborated with William Ernest Hocking on the volume *Types of Philosophy*.

J. H. GOLDSTEIN, Candler Professor of Chemistry. Ph.D., Harvard University, 1949. Dr. Goldstein has done extensive research in spectroscopy and theoretical chemistry, and has a special interest in scientific methodology.

HELMUT SCHOECK, Associate Professor of Sociology. Ph.D., University of Tübingen, 1948. Dr. Schoeck is the author of many books published in this country and abroad, including *Was heisst politisch unmöglich*, and *U.S.A.: Motive und Strukturen*.

WALTER D. LOVE, Assistant Professor of History. Ph.D., University of California at Berkeley, 1956. Dr. Love makes historiography and modern English history his major fields of research. He has recently published several articles on Irish historians, Irish historical materials, and Edmund Burke.

WALTER A. STRAUSS, Associate Professor of Romance Languages. Ph.D., Harvard University, 1951. Dr. Strauss is the author of *Proust and Literature,* has finished a volume on contemporary French drama, and is currently writing on Orphism in modern literature.

ROBERT L. SCRANTON, formerly Chairman of the Department of Classics and Professor of Classics, is now Professor of Classical Archaeology at the University of Chicago. Ph.D., University of Chicago, 1939. Dr. Scranton has published two volumes on the excavations at Corinth, a book on Greek architecture, and has completed a manuscript on the arts of the ancient Mediterranean world.

LEROY E. LOEMKER, Candler Professor of Philosophy. Ph.D., Boston University, 1931. Dr. Loemker has published a translation and edition of the *Philosophical Papers and Letters* of Leibniz.

WARD PAFFORD, Professor of English. Ph.D., Duke University, 1950. Dr. Pafford is especially interested in early nineteenth-century English literature and has published several articles in this field.

GREGOR SEBBA, Professor, Graduate Institute of the Liberal Arts. *Dr. rer. pol., Dr. utr. iur.,* University of Innsbruck, 1927, 1929. Dr. Sebba has published widely in fields ranging from economics to comparative literature. He has published critical bibliographies of Descartes and Malebranche and is currently writing a book on the nature of aesthetic creativity.

SPECTRUM PAPERBACKS

OTHER SPECTRUM BOOKS . . . *quality paper-backs that meet the highest standards of scholarship and integrity.*

* Also available in limited clothbound edition.

*The American Assembly Series**

* Also available in limited clothbound edition.

Classics in History Series*

Science and Technical Series*

Twentieth Century Views Series*

* Also available in limited clothbound edition.